STRAND PRICE
1.00

FRENCH COMPOSITION

BY

L. RAYMOND TALBOT, A.M.

INSTRUCTOR IN FRENCH IN BOSTON UNIVERSITY
AUTHOR OF "LE FRANÇAIS ET SA PATRIE"

οὐ πόλλ' ἀλλὰ πολύ

BENJ. H. SANBORN & CO.
CHICAGO   NEW YORK   BOSTON
1916

Copyright, 1915,
By BENJ. H. SANBORN & CO.

FOREWORD

THE author hopes these exercises will prove interesting. They aim to give to descriptions of French life and scenes the human touch too often lacking in composition texts. Entertainment cannot, however, be the main consideration. To be useful, exercises must be *practical*.

The word *practical*, as used here, means this: Exercises must supply *abundant* practice in the *use* of *all* constructions which the pupil studies. It is futile, for instance, to make him study partitive articles, and then include only two or three partitives in the corresponding exercises. Only when such constructions are abundant can the pupil learn to apply his rules correctly.

Each lesson contains three sections. Section *A* consists of detached sentences affording copious illustrative material. *B* and *C* are in connected prose, but abound in the constructions the pupil has been studying. *C* is somewhat more difficult than *B* and may be used either for additional practice, for alternate exercises, or for a second review course. In general it may be said that lessons can be readily divided, the order of sections changed, and the work otherwise adapted to the needs of the class.

At the head of each lesson are given topics for grammatical study. No rules are printed, but subjects are assigned such as are treated in any good grammar. In the later lessons references are more and more frequent to subjects for which little time has been available in regular class work. The object is to send the pupil to the grammar, that he may form the habit of finding out things for himself.

Notes are brief and to the point. They are placed at the end of each lesson because a large majority of teachers prefer them there. The arrangement is sufficiently convenient in the preparation of the lesson, while not so convenient as to serve as a crutch in recitation.

There is no apology for the lesson which calls for French equivalents of the word *get*. Some may omit these sentences because they employ rather liberally our native colloquialisms. Yet it seems advisable to teach pupils how French expresses the ideas for which we overwork this little word.

Lesson X gives no facts regarding French geography, since any statement made now may be inaccurate at the close of the war. The lesson consists of questions on geography; the grammar assigned is on interrogative pronouns. Why not? Pupils are glad to learn the facts for themselves and to answer the questions in French!

Many composition texts follow corresponding readers too closely. This book is not based on the author's reader, "Le Français et sa Patrie." But in subject matter it covers the same ground, and accordingly references to the corresponding pages of the reader are given in parentheses in the heading of nearly every lesson. Teachers who wish to use the two books together, will find these references helpful. Teachers using the Composition independently will, of course, disregard them.

The author appreciates gratefully valuable help from Professor James Geddes, Jr., of Boston University; Miss Alice M. Twigg, of the Girls' High School, Boston; Miss Frances L. Hoyt, of the Everett (Mass.) High School; Miss Abbie I. Durkee, of the Malden (Mass.) High School; and Miss Laura G. Willgoose, of the Melrose (Mass.) High School.

L. R. TALBOT.

OCTOBER, 1915.

TABLE OF CONTENTS

	PAGE
FOREWORD	iii

EXERCISE I. THE ARRIVAL AT PARIS.
    Regular conjugations of verbs; *avoir* and *être;* partitive constructions; *depuis* with the present and imperfect indicative 1

EXERCISE II. A WALK IN PARIS.
    Orthographical peculiarities of the first conjugation; common uses of tenses; partitive constructions (continued); *aller, dire* 3

EXERCISE III. BREAKFAST, LUNCHEON, AND DINNER.
    Agreement of past participles; reflexive verbs; the idiom *venir de; s'en aller; venir, tenir, s'asseoir* 6

EXERCISE IV. AN AFTERNOON AT THE BOIS.
    Conjunctive personal pronouns; *mourir, voir* . . . 8

EXERCISE V. AT THE THEATER.
    Conjunctive personal pronouns (continued); *y* and *en; croire, partir,* and verbs similarly conjugated . . . 11

EXERCISE VI. THE POSTAL SYSTEM.
    Disjunctive personal pronouns; *mettre, ouvrir,* and verbs similarly conjugated 14

EXERCISE VII. FRENCH GOVERNMENT.
    Possessive pronouns and adjectives; *écrire, lire.*

EXERCISE VIII. THE PANTHEON AND SOME CHURCHES. 17
    Demonstrative pronouns and adjectives; *faire, conduire,* and verbs similarly conjugated 21

EXERCISE IX. BUYING BOOKS.
    Relative pronouns; *envoyer, vouloir* 24

TABLE OF CONTENTS

PAGE

EXERCISE X. A GEOGRAPHY LESSON.
Interrogative pronouns; *courir*, *recevoir*, and verbs similarly conjugated 28

EXERCISE XI. THE NATIONAL LIBRARY.
Indefinite pronouns; review of all pronouns; *pouvoir*, *savoir*, differences between these two verbs 31

EXERCISE XII. CHRISTMAS AND NEW YEAR'S DAY.
Numerals, dates, age, time of day; *valoir*, *naître* . . 34

EXERCISE XIII. STREET SCENES.
Numerals (continued); impersonal verbs; *pleuvoir*, *falloir* 38

EXERCISE XIV. THE WEATHER. HOW TO MAKE A FIRE.
Modal auxiliaries; uses of *devoir*; *devoir*, *craindre*, and verbs similarly conjugated 42

EXERCISE XV. ART AT PARIS.
Modal auxiliaries; uses of *devoir* (continued); *devoir*, *pouvoir*, *savoir*, *falloir*, *vouloir* 47

EXERCISE XVI. EDUCATION IN FRANCE.
Modal auxiliaries (continued); *connaître* and *savoir* and their uses 51

EXERCISE XVII. THE CARNIVAL.
Faire, *laisser*, *voir*, and *entendre*, with dependent infinitives; *faire*, *voir*, *suivre* 55

EXERCISE XVIII. VERSAILLES, ST. DENIS, AND CHARTRES.
Subjunctive after expressions of desiring, avoiding, commanding, forbidding, consenting; *plaire*, *boire* . . . 60

EXERCISE XIX. SPRING IN PARIS.
Subjunctive after expressions of approval or disapproval, emotion, or sentiment; *vaincre*, *prendre*, and verbs similarly conjugated 65

EXERCISE XX. THE MARKETS.
Subjunctive after expressions of doubt, denial, etc., and after expressions of perceiving, thinking, knowing, etc.; *faillir*, *fuir* 69

EXERCISE XXI. FONTAINEBLEAU.
Subjunctive in adjectival clauses, — clauses of character-

TABLE OF CONTENTS

	PAGE
istic, after a superlative, with "whoever," "whatever," etc.; *rire, vêtir*	74

EXERCISE XXII. MONT ST. MICHEL.

Subjunctive in adverbial clauses, — with conjunctions of time before which or up to which, conjunctions of purpose or result, condition, and concession, conjunctions of negative force, with *que* replacing other conjunctions; *taire, acquérir*   78

EXERCISE XXIII. BRITTANY AND NORMANDY.

Subjunctive in principal clauses, review of subjunctives; tenses used after *si*, meaning "if"; tenses used after *quand* and similar conjunctions; pleonastic *ne* after comparatives; *vivre, cueillir* 83

EXERCISE XXIV. THE LOIRE VALLEY. BACK IN PARIS.

Idioms to express the word "get"; "used to"; uses of the past anterior; predicative *le, la, les; en* meaning "its"; *mouvoir* and *émouvoir, coudre* 87

EXERCISE XXV. FAIRS. THINGS TO SEE IN PARIS.

Idioms to express the word "take"; conditional sentences contrary to fact; *quand*, etc., with the conditional in the sense of a past future; *aller, envoyer, acquérir, courir, cueillir, faillir, fuir, haïr, prendre, conduire* . . . 92

EXERCISE XXVI. ON THE BANKS OF THE SEINE.

Idioms to express the words "put" and "marry"; idioms to express "hot," "cold," etc.; *pour* with the infinitive; *en* with the present participle; comparatives; verbs conjugated with *être; mourir, ouvrir, partir, tenir, venir, vêtir* . . 96

EXERCISE XXVII. WHAT THEY EAT AT PARIS.

Negatives; verbs governing dependent infinitives, and the prepositions that they require; verbs governing complements in ways different from English, such as *obéir à, s'approcher de, regarder, payer;* prepositions after verbs, such as *savoir gré de, penser à; conduire, connaître, coudre, craindre, croire*   100

EXERCISE XXVIII. MOTHER MICHEL. THE TWO AMERICANS WHO LOST THEIR WAY.

Prepositions governing infinitives (continued); words of

TABLE OF CONTENTS

nationality; numerals, expressions of measure; uses and omission of the articles; uses of the past anterior; *dire, écrire, faire, lire, mettre, moudre, naître, plaire, prendre, résoudre* 106

EXERCISE XXIX. MARSEILLES.

Uses of numerals in arithmetic, etc.; days of week, dates, etc.; uses of prepositions with adjectives, such as "good to eat," "good to him"; various uses of prepositions, with shades of meaning; *rire, suivre, vaincre, vivre, recevoir, devoir, asseoir, falloir, mouvoir* 111

EXERCISE XXX. TARASCON.

Uses of prepositions (continued); idioms to express personal appearance, such as "he has black eyes"; the word "since"; *depuis* and *il y a* with *ne*; *en* with the present participle; *pleuvoir, pouvoir, savoir, valoir, voir, vouloir* . 115

VOCABULARY 121

FRENCH COMPOSITION

EXERCISE I

THE ARRIVAL AT PARIS (Pages 1–6)

Grammatical study: regular conjugations of verbs; *avoir* and *être;* partitive constructions; *depuis* with the present and imperfect indicative.

A. 1. Have you any friends in this country? No, I haven't any friends in France. I am a [1] foreigner.

2. Most people who travel in France visit many beautiful cathedrals.

3. How many days have you been in [2] Paris? I have been here three weeks.

4. There are a great many boarding-houses in Paris.

5. How many years have you been studying French? I have been studying it only one year.

6. Do you speak French? Yes, sir, but not very well.

7. He has some French books. Have you any? No, I have none, but here are some English books.

8. My father speaks French very well. He has visited France many times.

9. We found some good boarding-houses in Switzerland.

10. How many compartments are there in this car? There are six.

B. Our friends left Switzerland a week ago. They have been in France for a week now, but they have not yet reached Paris, for they stopped at Dijon, a pretty city on the way from Geneva to the capital. There are many interesting cities in this country; some are worth visiting,[3] for their cathedrals and museums and for other buildings. But Paris is the largest and the most important city in [4] France.

Most people who travel in foreign countries speak English. Our friends met some gentlemen who had been studying French for years; yet they always found hotels where they met many people who spoke English. It is too bad. There are so many hotels where only French is spoken,[5] and where an American cannot hear his own language! And there are excellent pensions, too. Our friends used to live in boarding-houses when they were in Switzerland.

C. We had been traveling for several weeks in Switzerland. At last we had left this beautiful country and had started for Paris, the [1] capital of France and one of the most interesting cities in [4] the world. We longed to see this beautiful city. So, while we were very sorry to leave the mountains and lakes, still we were ready to visit new countries. We had taken a train at Geneva; we had found a compartment where we could [6] be alone. Then some Americans who, like us, were going to Paris to study French, came into our car. We were glad enough [7] to meet them; for when one is traveling in a foreign country he is always glad to find some people who live in [2] the United States. We talked for two or three hours, then being tired, we began to read.

We had been reading only a few minutes when the

customs official came into our compartment to inspect our baggage.[8] I had nothing to declare, but my friend had a little Swiss milk chocolate. It is better to tell the inspector if one has chocolate or lace; for there is a duty on these things. Especially one must not take any matches of foreign make into France, for the manufacture of [9] matches is controlled by the government. But since we had only a [1] very little chocolate, and no matches or [10] lace, the inspector said we needn't [11] pay anything.

About three o'clock we arrived at Paris. Of course, we were glad to get out of the train after our long journey. We took a subway train and went directly to a boarding-house, where my friends lived a year ago, when they were passing a few weeks here. Here I am at last, settled in [2] Paris! Everything seems strange, but later I shall get accustomed to the subways and the boulevards, the gardens and the parks.

1. omit. 2. *à*. 3. trans. *merit a visit*. 4. *de*. 5. use *on*. 6. tense? 7. *bien*. 8. plural. 9. the. 10. *ni*. 11. imp. *falloir*.

EXERCISE II

A WALK IN PARIS (Pages 9–21)

Grammatical study: orthographical peculiarities of the first conjugation; common uses of tenses; partitive constructions (continued); *aller, dire*.

A. 1. My friend says that when he was in Paris he used to eat a lot of milk chocolate.

FRENCH COMPOSITION

2. How many students are there at Paris? There are a great many.

3. You say that many students live in the Latin quarter.

4. He was commencing to [1] write letters to some friends.

5. This part of the city is called [2] the Left Bank. These gentlemen say [3] they are going to visit some friends who live here.

6. We are eating some rolls. We were going to give you some, but you have enough.

7. The king has been reigning for many years. Will he reign for a long time still?

8. If the man buys this horse, he will have four. He bought two yesterday.

9. What would he say if you told him this?

10. We are going to the square that used to be called Parvis-Notre-Dame.

B. How many interesting things there are to see in this city! One might [4] spend whole weeks in the churches and the museums. There are many places which are mentioned [5] in [6] literature. When one goes to the Ile de la Cité he sees [7] at once a large building with two square towers. Without asking [8] any questions he knows that it is the great cathedral of Notre-Dame. Hugo has told us the story of Quasimodo in his novel, Notre-Dame de Paris. Every statue calls to our minds [9] some historic event. Here is one which shows Roland, the great chief who conquered [10] the Moors. He is on horseback. The Sainte-Chapelle, a part of the court-house, with [1] the beautiful Gothic steeple and the splendid stained-glass windows, is also on [11] the island.

customs official came into our compartment to inspect our baggage.[8] I had nothing to declare, but my friend had a little Swiss milk chocolate. It is better to tell the inspector if one has chocolate or lace; for there is a duty on these things. Especially one must not take any matches of foreign make into France, for the manufacture of [9] matches is controlled by the government. But since we had only a [1] very little chocolate, and no matches or [10] lace, the inspector said we needn't [11] pay anything.

About three o'clock we arrived at Paris. Of course, we were glad to get out of the train after our long journey. We took a subway train and went directly to a boarding-house, where my friends lived a year ago, when they were passing a few weeks here. Here I am at last, settled in [2] Paris! Everything seems strange, but later I shall get accustomed to the subways and the boulevards, the gardens and the parks.

1. omit. 2. *à*. 3. trans. *merit a visit*. 4. *de*. 5. use *on*. 6. tense? 7. *bien*. 8. plural. 9. the. 10. *ni*. 11. imp. *falloir*.

EXERCISE II

A WALK IN PARIS (Pages 9–21)

Grammatical study: orthographical peculiarities of the first conjugation; common uses of tenses; partitive constructions (continued); *aller, dire*.

A. 1. My friend says that when he was in Paris he used to eat a lot of milk chocolate.

2. How many students are there at Paris? There are a great many.

3. You say that many students live in the Latin quarter.

4. He was commencing to [1] write letters to some friends.

5. This part of the city is called [2] the Left Bank. These gentlemen say [3] they are going to visit some friends who live here.

6. We are eating some rolls. We were going to give you some, but you have enough.

7. The king has been reigning for many years. Will he reign for a long time still?

8. If the man buys this horse, he will have four. He bought two yesterday.

9. What would he say if you told him this?

10. We are going to the square that used to be called Parvis-Notre-Dame.

B. How many interesting things there are to see in this city! One might [4] spend whole weeks in the churches and the museums. There are many places which are mentioned [5] in [6] literature. When one goes to the Ile de la Cité he sees [7] at once a large building with two square towers. Without asking [8] any questions he knows that it is the great cathedral of Notre-Dame. Hugo has told us the story of Quasimodo in his novel, Notre-Dame de Paris. Every statue calls to our minds [9] some historic event. Here is one which shows Roland, the great chief who conquered [10] the Moors. He is on horseback. The Sainte-Chapelle, a part of the court-house, with [1] the beautiful Gothic steeple and the splendid stained-glass windows, is also on [11] the island.

We went to the cathedral this morning. We went up into the towers to [12] enjoy the view of [13] the city. This afternoon we are going to take a walk in the parks, but of course we wanted to take our first walk in the oldest part of the city.

C. The janitress is sweeping the stairs. I am going to wait a few minutes, for I have some questions which I want to ask her.[14] First, I wish to know what is happening at the *mairie*, across the street. Then, I want to know if she has any letters for me. At present I have hardly any money; I am always glad to receive letters when I am traveling, but from time to time, especially when I need money, I can hardly wait for the postman to come.[15] Oh, here is the janitress. "Excuse me, madame, but are there any letters for me? I believe there is an American mail to-day." — "Yes, sir, you are right; the postman has just come,[16] and here are two letters for you; there are some for your friend, too."

If I had money enough, I should like to stay longer in Paris. I can stay here only a few weeks. I have been here only since last night, but I am beginning already to feel the charm of this old city. I am going to take advantage of the time that I shall have here, and [12] see as many things as possible.

1. *à*. 2. *s'appeler*. 3. insert *that*. 4. *pourrait*. 5. of which (*dont*) one makes mention. 6. the. 7. *voit*. 8. inf. 9. calls to us to the mind. 10. *vainquit*. 11. *dans*. 12. *pour*. 13. *sur*. 14. ind. obj. 15. subjunctive. 16. *arriver*.

EXERCISE III

BREAKFAST, LUNCHEON AND DINNER (Pages 7–8; 21–24; 38–41)

Grammatical study: agreement of past participles; reflexive verbs; the idiom *venir de; s'en aller; venir, tenir, s'asseoir*.

A. 1. We got up at seven o'clock this morning and we came here before eating [1] our [2] breakfast.

2. They went away this morning, but they will come back later, for they have just arrived in Paris.

3. When she arrived, her mother had just read the letters which the janitor had brought.

4. Sit down. Eat these cakes which the maid has brought.

5. He is buying a new house. When he [3] and his wife have settled in it,[4] they want [5] us to go [6] and [7] visit [1] them.

6. How many rolls has the maid brought? There aren't any here, for she hasn't come yet.

7. She is holding in [8] her hand the two books which she procured yesterday.

8. She gets up at seven every day. She went to bed late last night.

9. When we had settled in Paris we soon got accustomed to speaking [1] French.

10. When we arrived they were already sitting at the table.

B. We took a walk yesterday; then, as we had some letters to write, we didn't go to bed until [9] midnight. So we woke [10] up quite late. We got up at once. We were ready to eat the rolls and coffee which the maid had already brought. In France one eats only very little for [2] breakfast. The family doesn't come together for this meal, but each person has rolls and coffee, or chocolate, or perhaps milk, in his room. After dressing [11] (for we have already got accustomed to the French habit of eating [1] breakfast before dressing [1]) we went out. It was [12] splendid weather, and we went to the Champs-Elysées.

When we came back at noon we were tired and hungry. Luncheon was ready. We sat down at once. We had meat and potatoes and then some cheese and some jam. These French jams are delicious. We were glad to [13] have some butter, for they [14] don't have it [15] with all the meals. But there is no salt in this butter.

After luncheon we stayed a few minutes and were introduced to Mrs. B's brother, who had just come in as we were finishing the meal.

C. Well, Madame, we have come back in time. We hurried, for we knew that you wouldn't sit down without us. — Where did you go this afternoon? — We went to the Champs-Elysées; everybody was there! — Let's sit down at once; for the soup is ready, and it will be cold if we don't eat it soon. — Give me the salt and pepper, please. Thank you. — We have a leg of lamb this evening and some peas. — Will you give me another [16] glass of water? Thank you. — Let me give you a little more [17] meat and some more [17] potatoes. — This salad is very good. — What sort of fruit do you prefer? Here are some oranges and some figs. The figs are just as they were picked, not dry like those that you eat in America. Help yourself [18] to the crackers. May I offer you something more? — No, thank you, Madame; I have all I need.[19] Now we must [19] leave you, for we have some more letters to write, and as soon as we have finished them we shall go to bed. Good night, Madame. — Good night, Gentlemen.

1. inf. 2. the. 3. *lui*. 4. *y*. 5. *veulent*. 6. subjunctive. 7. omit. 8. *à*. 9. *ne ... qu'à*. 10. inverted order. 11. perf. inf. 12. *faisait un*. 13. *de*. 14. *on*. 15. part. 16. *encore un;* why not *un autre?* 17. *encore*. 18. *se servir*. 19. *falloir*.

EXERCISE IV

AN AFTERNOON AT THE BOIS (Pages 25-38)

Grammatical study: conjunctive personal pronouns; *mourir, voir*.

A. 1. He is bringing her some beautiful flowers. He tells me that he found them in the Bois de Boulogne.

2. We shall see them when they come to-morrow. He sent them yesterday.

3. They were coming this morning; but we told them that we should not see them, for we should not be here.

4. The king and queen died a year ago. Did you ever see them?

5. They are holding French flags. Where did they find them? Who gave them to them?

6. Our friend who died gave us that painting. I used to see it every time that I went to his house.

7. My father wants [1] to read that book. When you have finished it, bring it to him, if you please.

8. They will die in prison. You will see them when you go there to-morrow.

9. Keep your tickets. When the inspector comes, show them to him.

10. As soon as she had bought them, she showed them to us.

B. Let's take a walk this afternoon. It is [2] fine weather, and it's better [3] to be outdoors than to [4] visit the museums. — Where are we going? — Let's go to the Bois de Boulogne. You will see a great [5] many people there, and it is a beautiful place. — Shall we see the Champs-Elysées and the Tuileries Gardens [6] on the way? — Yes, we shall cross them.

Here is the Seine. You saw it this morning. You were speaking a few minutes ago of the Tuileries Gardens. Here they are. — Aren't those flowers beautiful! — Yes, and they are beautiful until [7] November, for the climate is mild, and it is [2] only rarely cold. — What is the wide avenue which I see off there? — Why,[8] that's the Avenue des Champs-Elysées. You don't recognize [9] it when you see it! We are now in [10] the Place de la Concorde; look at it well, for it's one of the most beautiful squares in [4] the world. It is in [10] this square that many people were killed on the guillotine, during the Revolution. — What are those great trees on either side [11] of the avenue? — They [12] are chestnut trees; when they are in blossom, the avenue is very beautiful.

Here we are at the Bois. It [12] is not a large forest, but

there are places here where one can forget that he is so
near a big city.—I am starving; aren't you hungry,
too?—Yes, let's buy something to eat. But let's not
buy it at [13] the restaurant; everything costs too much [14]
there, and we're not rich. Let's buy it at [13] that little
shop.

C. This afternoon we went to the Bois. On the way
we saw a great crowd of people beyond the Place de la
Concorde. I wondered what it was. I went up to a
policeman and I said to him: "Excuse me, what is that
crowd?" "Oh, Monsieur, that's Guignol," he said.
"Tell me, please, what's a Guignol?" Then he explains
to me that it is a sort of show in which the actors are
dummies. He was surprised that I had [15] never seen them.
I told him that we had just come to Paris for the first
time. Then we thanked him. We were much interested
in [16] the show and in the children who were having such a
good time.

After staying at the Bois an hour, and after going boating, we took a street car to come back to the house. I was
starving, for I had had nothing to eat all the afternoon.
We might have walked if we had had [17] time, and we
should have enjoyed the walk, for it is in a beautiful part
of the city. But it was getting [18] late. I had never been in
a French street car. The conductor gave us some tickets
when we had given him our money. When he gave them
to us I thought [19] it was [5] a funny idea.[20] But an Englishman who was behind us explained to me that if we
didn't keep the tickets, to show them when the conductor
came in,[21] we should have to pay for our ride again.

FRENCH COMPOSITION 11

Then I decided that it was worth while to keep them. There's a reason for everything that you see at Paris!

1. *veut.* 2. *faire.* 3. *vaut mieux.* 4. *de.* 5. omit. 6. Gardens of the Tuileries. 7. *jusqu'en.* 8. *mais.* 9. *reconnaissez.* 10. *sur.* 11. *de chaque côté.* 12. *ce.* 13. *dans.* 14. too dear. 15. subjunctive. 16. *à.* 17. the. 18. *se faire.* 19. *trouver.* 20. *une drôle d'idée.* 21. cond.; why?

EXERCISE V

AT THE THEATER (Pages 41-47)

Grammatical study: conjunctive personal pronouns (continued); *y* and *en; croire, partir,* and verbs similarly conjugated.

A. 1. Believe me; I tell you they have gone.

2. I believe you, but I thought they wouldn't use the tickets that we bought for them.

3. I think he is sleeping now. Don't wake him.

4. He will get up soon, and I will tell him that you have come to see him.

5. I thought they would come back soon. When you see them, give them this.

6. If you see him, shall you give it to him?

7. She wants you to buy her some tickets.

8. I have sent her some already. Tell her to[1] use them.

9. She used them. But she went to sleep during the first act!

10. Who told you so[2]? I saw her.

11. I am surprised that you should believe[3] her when she tells you she was there.

12. I didn't see her there. I tell you she didn't go.

13. I am buying them some tickets.

14. Tell me, do you want me to buy you some?

15. Yes, buy me some, please.

16. I sent them some last week, but they didn't use them.

17. Sleep well; when you have waked up, get up at once.

18. I hope you will wake up early.

19. Go out. Wait for [4] me. I shall come out in a minute.

20. We shall see them if we wait for [4] them.

B. Let's see if they [5] are playing *Le Voyage de M. Perrichon* at the Comédie Française to-night. — What's [6] the Comédie Française? — Why, that's [7] the famous theater where Molière played, and where they give performances of the great classic plays, as well as of the best modern plays. — Is it far from here? — It is near the Louvre, on the right bank of the river. I think you have seen it. There's an advertising post; let's go over [4] there. We shall see on it the announcements of all the plays that are being given in Paris now. We must [8] see some. — *Le Voyage de M. Perrichon* is announced. — Yes, I'm glad of it, for it's a very amusing play, and I want you to see it. You remember that our teacher told us to see it if we had a [9] chance. — I have never read [10] it; shall I understand it when I see it at the theater? — I will tell you the story of it before we go.[11] Then you will understand the greater part of it.

We will go to the theater to buy our tickets, then we'll

FRENCH COMPOSITION 13

come back to the house for luncheon. — What, can we get good seats for to-night's performance? — Oh, yes. There are always some even up to [12] the time for [13] the curtain. People form in line then, for the tickets that are left are sold [14] at reduced prices. But I prefer to get my tickets ahead of time, — "en location," to use the French expression.

C. Last evening we went to the theater. We saw *Le Voyage de M. Perrichon*. It was my first visit at a French theater, and I saw there many things which seemed strange to me. For example, they sell the programs. The waits between the acts are longer than in our theaters in America. They didn't begin until [15] 8.30, and I am told that sometimes the curtain goes up [16] even later. We started from the house early, for we were anxious to see the people enter.

After leaving the theater, we went to the boulevards. It was late, and we were so tired that if we had come back to the house at once, I should have gone to sleep without any [17] difficulty. But we should have lost a good chance to see the French people. After leaving the theaters, everybody goes to [18] the restaurants which are along the boulevards; people amuse themselves there for a long time. We stayed there until half-past twelve,[19] and when we came away, there were still so many people that one would hardly have believed that it was a half hour after midnight.

To-morrow night we shall see *L'Oiseau Bleu*, Maeterlinck's beautiful play. But I think we shall come home as soon as we leave the theater; one night a [20] week is

14 FRENCH COMPOSITION

enough for me, to stay out so late. I prefer, usually, to go to bed a little earlier.

1. *de*, or *que* with subjunctive. 2. it. 3. pres. subjunctive. 4. omit. 5. *on*. 6. *qu'est-ce que c'est que*. 7. *c'est*. 8. *devons*. 9. the. 10. *lu*. 11. use inf. 12. *jusqu'à*. 13. *de*. 14. refl. 15. not until = only at. 16. rises. 17. *aucune*. 18. *dans*. 19. midnight. 20. *par*.

EXERCISE VI

THE POSTAL SYSTEM (Pages 52–54)

Grammatical study: disjunctive personal pronouns; *mettre, ouvrir*, and verbs similarly conjugated.

A. 1. He has offered you some postage stamps for your collection.

2. How much did he pay for [1] them?

3. He and I wanted to get some, but there weren't any.

4. Send me some to-morrow. Don't offer him any.

5. He introduced her to him.

6. Introduce me to her, please; to her, not to him.

7. You and she went with him to the post office.

8. Is she thinking of him now?

9. Let's approach them. Let's offer them some money.

10. Come to me when you need me.

11. Bring me some postage stamps, please; don't send them to me.

12. I haven't any; I used them this morning.

13. Here they are; I have bought you some.

14. I got two of them, too. I think we have enough.

15. She and her mother have gone out.

16. They are leaving at ten o'clock. They didn't put on[1] their hats. Who went out with them?

17. Who opened the door? I.

18. Who put those books there? He. If I had put them there, I should tell you so.

19. I want you and him to put these boxes on the table. When you have opened them, put them under the table.

20. Open them there. When I tell you,[2] cover them with your[3] hands.

B. I have written so many letters since arriving[4] at Paris, that I had no more stamps this morning, and my friend and I went to the post office. He went with me, for I have been in Paris only a few days and had never seen the sign, "Office of Posts, Telegraphs and Telephones," which is so well known to him.[5] On the way he explained to me the French postal[6] system. I asked[7] him many questions. How many deliveries of letters are there a[8] day? There are seven, except Sundays and holidays, when there are three, in[1] the morning. He told me that there was an excellent parcel post system; they have had it for many years, so that France is ahead of the United States, since we have had this part of the postal service only a short[9] time. Then I saw a box which bore the sign, "Pneumatic Service," and my friend explained it to me. If you are in a hurry, you put a six-cent stamp[10] on the letter, and put it in this special box; it goes by a pneumatic tube, and within very little time a messenger takes it to the address. You can even send a card for the answer, which comes to you within an hour. This service, of course, holds good only within the city. The government owns the telephone and telegraph system, also.

My friend and I bought some stamps. Madame had told me that she needed some two-cent stamps, and had asked me to [11] get some for her. When I opened my purse, I found that I had only one franc, not enough to pay for [1] all the stamps [12] I had bought. But my friend paid for them for me.

C. Charles has just received a letter from his cousin, in the United States. There was only a two-cent stamp on the letter, so that he had to pay six cents [13] "postage due." Why do our American friends never remember that it takes [14] a five-cent stamp to send a letter to foreign countries, except Germany and Great Britain? (Let's not forget Canada, Mexico, and Cuba, too.) Then, when the letters have arrived here in Paris, *we*, who are so poor that we have to look at each two-cent piece twice before spending it, have to pay six cents, or twice the amount that is lacking. Charles says he's going to write to his cousin and tell him that he has suffered a long time from [11] his lack of foresight, that he wants *him* (that is,[15] the cousin) to learn the price of stamps for France. (That sentence is rather long and complicated, but that's the way [16] *he* told *me*.[2])

When the postman came this morning, he brought *me* a letter, too. When I opened it, I was surprised to [11] find in it a photograph of [17] Charles and me in the Alps. An American lady whom we had met in Switzerland had taken [7] it. I was glad to [11] hear from her.[18] I have some postal cards and I am going to send her one, to let[7] her know that the letter containing [19] the photograph has just arrived. I shall thank her for [11] having thought of me, and for having sent me this photograph. I was thinking of it yesterday and I was wondering if it was good.[20]

1. omit. 2. it. 3. the. 4. my arrival. 5. conj. pers. pron., ind. obj. 6. of the posts. 7. *faire*. 8. *par*. 9. *peu*. 10. stamp of six cents. 11. *de*. 12. which. 13. of. 14. *falloir*. 15. *c'est-à-dire*. 16. it's like that that. 17. which showed. 18. have of her news. 19. which contains. 20. *ressemblante*.

EXERCISE VII

FRENCH GOVERNMENT (Pages 58-64)

Grammatical study: possessive pronouns and adjectives; *écrire, lire.*

A. 1. My mother is writing a letter to yours.

2. She has just been reading the letter which your mother wrote to her.

3. Your sister is reading your brother's exercises and mine.

4. His are better written than mine.

5. Describe your photographs and his.

6. This book is mine; it isn't hers.

7. Their mother has hurt her right hand.

8. When she writes [1] letters, she will use her left hand.

9. She has broken her arm.

10. She wants [2] you to write some letters for her.

11. They used to elect a mayor every year, but now they elect one only every [3] four years.

12. I read that in your newspapers.

13. Who wrote the books which you read last summer in [4] the country?

14. Your father wanted [5] you to read his.

15. Let us write to him. He never reads any good books.

16. Let us tell him that if he should read [6] good books, he would profit much by it.[7]

17. When she had read the letters that you and I had written to her, she started at once for the city.

18. Your letters are more interesting than mine.

19. His books are larger than yours.

20. Before he writes,[8] let him hold his hands in front of the fire.

B. France has been a republic less than [9] fifty years. Twice before, there had been a republic for a short [10] time. In 1848, Napoleon was elected president, but in 1850 he became emperor. Then in 1871, after the Franco-Prussian war, the present republic was formed.[11]

There are some important differences between the government of France and that of our country. In the United States, we elect a president for four years; or rather, we, the voters, choose the electoral college, which in [4] its turn elects the president. But we are really choosing the president. In France it is [12] the Senate and the House of Deputies that elect the president. Here he is elected for four years; there he is at the head of the government for [13] seven years.

In America, there are forty-eight states, which are really little republics themselves, each [14] independent in many things. In France the country is divided [11] into [15] eighty-six departments, but the government is centralized. The prefect, who governs the department, has relatively little power; he is under the orders of the central government. Each one [14] of these departments is divided [11] into [15] arrondissements, while [16] these are subdivided [11] into [15] cantons, then each canton into communes. Each commune has its mayor.

One thing seems strange. A man who wishes to be elected to the House of Deputies can choose the department which he wishes to represent. It is not necessary for him to live [17] there. Provided he owns property [18] there, he can be a candidate.

C. Paris contains twenty arrondissements. Its population is so large that with two neighboring cities it forms a department. At the head of the government in Paris there is a prefect, as in [19] all the other departments. As for the arrondissements of Paris, their government is different from that of the other arrondissements. Ordinarily they are governed by sub-prefects, while those at [20] Paris have mayors.

In France, the president has a council, which resembles the cabinet of our presidents. There, the president of the republic chooses the president of the council, and *he* appoints his colleagues; if the president of the republic approves the choice, they become ministers. There are twelve of them. It is not important to [20] know the different ministries.

20 FRENCH COMPOSITION

Formerly, in[4] the Middle Ages, France was made up of a great number of provinces, the names of which are still heard in [21] conversation. For example, there were Normandy, Brittany, Provence. The inhabitants of these provinces were called Normans, Bretons, Provençaux, and so on. These names are all that remains of old governments which were formerly independent, but which later the kings of France conquered. One hears these province names from time to time, especially those of some of the most famous provinces, as [22] Brittany and Normandy, but they have no meaning so far as the government is concerned.[23]

There are still a few people in France who would like to see reëstablished the kingdom of the time of the Louis, and some who hope that the empire will return, as under Napoleon I and his nephew, Louis-Napoleon. Nearly everyone, however, is loyal to the present republic, especially since the beginning of the war of 1914.

M. Raymond Poincaré is president at the present time. He was elected in 1913.

1. what tense? 2. *veut* + pres. subjunctive. 3. all the. 4. *à*. 5. *a voulu* + imp. subj. 6. imp. ind. 7. by = *de*; *de* + it = ? 8. pres. subj. 9. *de;* why? 10. *peu*. 11. refl. 12. plural. 13. *pendant*. 14. use pronominal form. 15. *en*. 16. *tandis que*. 17. pres. subj. 18. to own property = *être propriétaire;* pres. subj. 19. *pour*. 20. *de*. 21. the. 22. insert *of*. 23. for that which concerns the government.

EXERCISE VIII

THE PANTHEON AND SOME CHURCHES (Pages 25, 26, 30, 47-52)

Grammatical study: demonstrative pronouns and adjectives; *faire*, *conduire*, and verbs similarly conjugated.

A. 1. The ones who did this have gone away.

2. What will these men do, when those who are destroying these buildings have gone away?

3. Translate this lesson; this one, not that one.

4. You have already translated that one, haven't you? I am translating it now.

5. Take this man to the new church.

6. He wishes to see the one that is being built [1] on the site of that old house.

7. These gloves are mine. Where are yours?

8. Those that are on the table, and the silk ones which she has in her hand, are hers.

9. Those who would do such a thing ought to be led out of the city and driven away.

10. Did any one see that?

11. I was destroying my old papers, — the ones on which I had translated my lessons.

12. When shall you translate this lesson and the one that your father wants you to translate?

13. This lesson is harder than that one.

14. I want you to make a list of the new words that you find [2] in it.

15. This is my father.

16. The man who is making that table is my uncle.

17. I want to introduce you to him and to the one who has just come in.

18. He is protecting those who need aid.

19. These men are sick, while [3] those are the ones whose [4] houses have been destroyed by the fire.

20. Take these men [5] to the doctor's; I will help those men,[5] myself.

B. I have made a list of the most important churches and other public buildings. These are the ones that we have already visited. I want you to take me to those that I have not yet seen. — All right; let's begin to-day. Let me see this list. It is such a fine day,[6] let us take a long walk and go to some of these places. What! You haven't seen the Madeleine? That's one of the most beautiful churches in [7] Paris. It is more modern than the most of those [8] you have seen. It is very near the Place de la Concorde. — I want to see again the one which we passed the other day, St. Germain-des-Prés; you told me that they destroyed part of it to [9] make the boulevard. — Yes, it is an interesting old church. Its nave is especially old. It has an interesting historical connection, for at the time of the Revolution many priests were shut up there. They say that these priests had a secret passage leading [10] from this church to the one which is called Notre-Dame-des-Champs.

Near the market there is a "temple"; that is what they call [11] the Protestant churches; this one is called l'Oratoire. Fénelon, one of the most famous [12] French preachers, used to preach here. I will take you there Sunday, if you wish.[13]

But let's go out. Make lists of the churches which we shall visit to-day, and of those which you want [13] to see later. We have mentioned only a few of those which you wish to see.

C. Yesterday, when we came out of the house, we had made our plans to [9] visit some of the old churches of Paris. But as soon as we had reached the street, we met some friends who were starting for the Pantheon, and they took us with them. I had not thought of that building, when I was making my list of churches. The Pantheon is not really a church, but it is a temple erected in memory of the great men of France by "the grateful fatherland." It is on the site of the church which formerly contained the tomb of St. Genevieve. I had never heard of her before going [14] to the Pantheon. She is the one [15] who protected Paris so many times, — at the time of a siege, again when there was a plague, and so on. She is the patron saint of Paris. She drove off Attila, king of the Huns, when he was threatening Paris, in [16] the fifth century. If he had been victorious, he would have destroyed the whole civilization of the west.

I became so interested in the history of St. Genevieve and in that of Joan of Arc that I hardly thought of the building itself or [17] of the vaults beneath it, where are the tombs of some of the great men. I spent most of the time looking at [18] the paintings which show scenes in the lives of these two saints. There are some representing [19] other scenes taken from [20] French history, but the ones which interested me most are those that show St. Genevieve.

We had hardly time to [21] go down into the cellar. But

I did have time to notice how respectful the French are [22] toward their heroes. All the men took off their hats [23] as they approached the tombs of these great men. I think that [24] is a lesson for us [25] Americans.

I shall go back to the Pantheon many times before I leave [14] Paris, I am sure, [26] for I want to study its pictures with more care, and the beautiful building is also well worth studying.[27]

1. use *on*. 2. fut. 3. *tandis que*. 4. *dont*; insert *the*. 5. use pron. 6. it is (makes) so fine to-day. 7. *de*; why? 8. insert *que*. 9. *pour*. 10. *qui menait*. 11. *c'est comme cela qu'on appelle*. 12. of the. 13. *voulez*. 14. inf. 15. *c'est elle*. 16. *à*. 17. *ni*. 18. *à* with inf. 19. which represent. 20. *dans*. 21. *le temps de*. 22. put the adj. after the verb. 23. *se découvrir*. 24. *voilà* or *c'est là*. 25. *nous autres*. 26. of it. 27. that one study it.

EXERCISE IX

BUYING BOOKS (Pages 54-58)

Grammatical study: relative pronouns; *envoyer, vouloir*.

A. 1. We have sent for [1] the men whom we met last year [2] in France.

2. Those who can will send us what they have done.

3. They are sending to the country the books [3] they have chosen.

4. I want you to send me the ones that you were reading when we came.

5. Those whose books have not come will buy some.

6. Here are the ones you need. Where are the ones in which you were reading yesterday?

7. The lady in whose house she lives has arrived.

8. She wants you to tell her what has happened and what you want her to do.

9. That is the lady with whose sister we went to the theater.

10. The one who introduced me to her is your father.

11. The city in which he lives is larger than the one [3] we wanted to visit.

12. I am sending you some post cards which show views of the latter.

13. These are the books of which I was thinking.

14. What I am thinking of, is [4] that you will want to see all that I have read. That is [5] why I am sending them to you.

15. The men [3] you were talking about want to see you.

16. I mean the ones with whose sons you used to go to school.

17. If I should send [6] her what I have written, would she read it?

18. Yes, and send her the pen with which you wrote it.

19. The man whose plays we have read is a Frenchman.

20. I should like to have him send [7] me the one which tells what Napoleon's son did [8] in Austria.

B. We have been in Paris three weeks, and I want to spend the morning picking out [9] books. Those that I shall buy to-day I shall send [10] to America to some of my friends who have never been in Europe. — Tell me what you want to buy; novels, plays, or something [11] else? —

A little of everything. I want some of these works about which you have been talking to me. — Let us start at once.

You can buy books very cheap here at Paris. Here are some that you want, Molière's plays, at ninety-five centimes, paper-covered, or at one franc ninety, bound in boards. — But I don't want to buy any paper-covered books; I prefer them bound. — I prefer to have them in paper,[12] for then I take them to the bookbinder's, [13] and he binds them for me [14]; thus all the books that I buy here will have the same binding.

All the books [3] you see here are classics. Those that are more recent are on these shelves, and cost more, naturally. Take what you want; they are willing for you to look over [15] the books as long as you wish.[16] When you are [16] ready, call the clerk and give him the ones you have [16] picked out.

I want to get a book on French literature in which I can [16] find all there is to know about the plays I have just read in school. — What you want is [4] Lanson's *Histoire de la littérature française*. It is the best book of the kind that there is.[17]

C. I have just returned from the bookseller's.[18] My friend and I spent the morning there buying books. Many of the French books that we have read in school are abridged editions, and I wanted to have them complete. So [19] I have spent nearly all my money.

Two of the books in [20] which I have been most interested are Hugo's novels, *Notre-Dame de Paris* and *Les Misérables*. They are two of the best stories that have ever been written,[21] either in French or in any [22] other language.

All that Hugo has written is worth reading, — his novels, his plays, his poems, his travel sketches, and the rest.

I am especially interested in French plays. The plays that I have read and those about which my teacher has told us have made me want to read as many as possible. So [19] I bought Molière's plays, those of Racine, and those of Corneille, as well as some by authors who are not so well known. I am very fond of Rostand's *Cyrano de Bergerac;* I have all his plays, also those of Maeterlinck; he, by the way, is a Belgian, although he lives most of the time in France.

I have mentioned only a few of the books that I have bought. They make a fine collection, of which I am rather proud, and which I shall want to show to all my friends when they come to see me.

A few of these books are bound in boards, but most French books are sold [23] in paper covers. Those that I have bought in paper covers, I shall send [10] to a bookbinder's, and he will bind them for me very cheap. I have a few second-hand books that I have found from time to time, and I shall have [24] these bound. Then all my French books will have the same binding.

1. *envoyer chercher.* 2. *l'année dernière* or *passée.* 3. the rel. pron., frequently omitted in English, must always be expressed in French. 4. *c'est.* 5. *voilà.* 6. imp. ind. 7. cond. of *vouloir* + pres. subj. 8. put subject after verb; why? 9. *à* + inf. 10. insert *them.* 11. insert *de.* 12. *brochés.* 13. *chez le relieur.* 14. use conj. pron. 15. *feuilleter.* 16. what tense? 17. pres. subj. 18. *de chez le . . .* 19. *aussi*, followed by verb and subject in inverted order. 20. *à.* 21. use *on;* subjunctive. 22. *toute.* 23. refl. 24. *faire* + inf.

EXERCISE X

A GEOGRAPHY LESSON (Pages 68-76)

Grammatical study: interrogative pronouns; *courir*, *recevoir*, and verbs similarly conjugated.

A. 1. Who is coming? What does he want?

2. Whom does he want to see? Who will receive him? What has he in [1] his hand?

3. With whom have they gone? What is going to happen?

4. Of what are you thinking? About whom are you speaking?

5. Whose hat is that? Whose child is he?

6. Whose house have you bought? Which house?

7. Who received the letter that he wrote?

8. What does he say? About what does he write?

9. What is that? What's La Manche?

10. What do you mean? If he received any letters, what would he do with [2] them?

11. Which man ran the fastest? The Frenchman. Which one?

12. When he receives the prize, what will he say?

13. Who teaches here? What does he teach?

14. Which language does he speak best? Which one does he prefer?

15. Who is that man who used to run [3] so fast every morning?

16. What was he doing? What is that noise?

17. Tell me what he means. What does he mean?

18. What is the cause of all that? Whom will you deceive with what you have said?

19. Whom do you expect to see?

20. What is that word that you used? Latitude? What is latitude?

B. Let us have a geography lesson.[4] Tell me what you know about France. What is its [5] population? What countries bound it? What countries are to the east? What ones to the north, the south, the west? You say there aren't any to the west. What is to the west of France? Which of these countries have you visited?

What are the most important cities of France? What is its capital? Which ones are seaports? What cities are on rivers?

Name the most important rivers in [6] the country.

What do you know about the manufactures of this country? What are its principal products? What are its industries? What is *culture maraîchère?* Explain its importance.

Are there any lakes in France? How many mountains are there?

Tell me what you know about the French people. What do you think of the Parisians, if you have ever met any? Of what do you think when one speaks to you about French culture? What is the *esprit français?*

For what is the city of Reims famous? What is made at Limoges? What has happened recently in Flanders? What do you think of what took place there?

Tell all you know about the French colonial possessions.

When you have done that, your geography lesson will be finished.

C. A few days ago the lady at whose house we live gave us a geography lesson. She told us a good [7] many things which seemed rather strange. All that you read in books about a country means only very little, but when you have visited even a part of the country, you are naturally much interested in all that you can learn concerning the customs of the people and their way of living.

We asked many questions of [1] the lady with whom we were discussing this subject. For instance: what was the area of the country, what was its population, and so on. When she began to use some of the strange names that I had never heard, I didn't understand all she said. "What is La Manche?", I asked her.[8] She explained very carefully all that I did not understand, and as she answered without any [9] difficulty all the questions we asked her, I am of the [7] opinion that she is well up on [10] geography.

What she told us about the climate of France surprised us a little. Although it is [11] in [12] about the same latitude as Canada, which means that it is much further [13] north than the part of the United States where my friend and I live, still its climate is much milder than that of the United States and Canada. This is because of the Gulf Stream.

Our friend told us that Mont Blanc was in France. At first we thought she was mistaken. "What," I said, "Mont Blanc in France? I thought it was [7] in Switzerland." "Why, no, it's in France, of course." "Which Mont Blanc?" — as if there were two of them! "The one you climbed last summer." I looked it up later and I found she was right. I had not remembered that Savoy, in which this mountain is situated, has belonged to France now for more than [6] fifty years.

1. *à.* 2. *de; de* + them = ? 3. what tense? 4. lesson of geography. 5. review the use of *en* in such cases as this. 6. *de;* why? 7. omit. 8. inverted order; why? 9. *aucune.* 10. *forte en.* 11. subj. 12. *sous.* 13. *plus.*

EXERCISE XI

THE NATIONAL LIBRARY (Pages 79–83)

Grammatical study: indefinite pronouns; review of all pronouns; *pouvoir, savoir,* differences between these two verbs.

A. 1. Whatever you say, nobody can ever believe you if he knows what you have just done.

2. You can do nothing which can [1] make him believe it.[2]

3. Who knows whether I can get a card for the library?

4. Do you know what is necessary? There is nobody here who can [1] help me.

5. He thought he could use books without paying anything.[3]

6. But what he was thinking of [4] is the National Library.

7. If you knew what the man about whom I am talking said to me yesterday, you could not ask such a question.

8. What can I do to help you? You cannot do anything.

9. I do not need anything. If I could help you, I should be very glad.[5]

10. None of the books that I have used belongs to me.

11. They were loaned to me. I have been using them for a week.

12. When he has learned all there is in those books, he will know how to write French.

13. What new thing is there?

14. There is nothing new, but we've just been told something very interesting.

15. What do you need?

16. What I need [4] is a dictionary, and I can't find one.

17. I cannot get along without it.

18. I have not been able to get one.

19. It may be that those who wrote this know how [1] to study, but I doubt it.[5]

20. They do not even know how to learn the regular verbs.

B. The National Library at Paris is one of the best libraries in the world. One who wants to study there can get an admission card without any difficulty and can study there every day without paying anything. He can use everything there is there. There are a great many dictionaries, encyclopedias, and other books of reference, which cost so much that those who are not rich cannot buy them. Anybody can take these books from [6] the cases without any formality.

If one wishes to use some book which is not in the open cases, he finds its number in the catalog, then he presents his slip at the office and the book is soon brought to him at his seat. Those who are studying French literature find so many books here that they might [7] stay here every day without even beginning to read all those in which they are interested, without saying anything of those that have less interest for them, but which they want to look over.

The collection of manuscripts which is in this library is very fine. For the man who is preparing an edition of some French masterpiece, and for *anybody* who is anxious to study literature thoroughly, these manuscripts are most important.[8] One who is interested in such things may well stay there many hours, looking them over.[9]

C. A certain American lady who had been living in Paris only a few weeks decided that she wished to study at the National Library. She had heard [10] of it, even before leaving [11] America, and she had read descriptions of it. She had been told that it was easy to get a card, and one morning, without saying anything to anybody, she set out. She knew what was necessary. So she started for the Prefecture of Police. She had heard it said so many times that the Paris police knew all who lived in Paris, and especially all the foreigners, that she knew they would give her what she desired; she was sure of it. But when she reached the offices, she found that nobody, of all who were working there, had ever heard [10] of her. She was told that she must prove that she was an American citizen. Now she had not thought of that! Didn't everybody know, without being told,[12] that she was an American? Ah yes, but she would have [13] to prove it, and for that she needed a paper signed by the consul.

I cannot tell you all the troubles she had before getting the card that she so much desired. She was sent from one office to another, and before she left [11] the building she was almost on the point of giving up all she had wanted to do. If she had known how to speak French, she might have got along more easily, for then she could have talked very pointedly,[14] and the clerk would have done what she asked without asking [15] her so many questions. She would have known, no doubt, that a little tip helps, even in government offices. It is well worth while to tip the man of whom you are asking help.

1. subj. 2. *le lui faire croire.* 3. *rien;* before inf. 4. it. 5. of it. 6. *dans.* 7. cond. 8. all that there is of most important. 9. *à* + inf. 10. insert *to speak.* 11. inf. 12. *sans que* + subj.; . . . *one tell it to him.* 13. cond. of *falloir* + pres. subj. 14. use *mettre les points sur les i.* 15. *faire* or *poser.*

EXERCISE XII

CHRISTMAS AND NEW YEAR'S DAY (Pages 87-90)

Grammatical study: numerals, dates, age, time of day; *valoir, naître.*

(All numbers are to be expressed in French words.)

A. 1. July 14 is a holiday in France.

2. On that day, more than 125 years ago, in 1789, the Bastille was destroyed.

3. This house is worth as much as that one.

4. When they are finished, the two will be worth more than 50,000 francs.

5. Some of the most important dates in French history

are 732, 800, 1066, 1648, 1789, 1793, 1804, 1815, 1870–71, 1914.

6. These years are important in the history of America: 1492, 1620, 1776, 1812, 1861–65, 1898, and 1914, when the Panama Canal [1] was opened.

7. His mother and his sister are both rich.

8. The latter has 500,000 francs, the mother has 286,500, and he has 2,000,000.

9. She was born on March 19, 1840.

10. She died the sixth of June, 1910.

11. She was a little more than 70 years old.

12. He is 19 years old.

13. He is three years older than his sister, but six years younger than his brother.

14. How old is the latter?

15. Several children are being born at [2] this very moment.

16. Thousands will be born while you are writing these exercises.

17. King Louis XIV was born in 1638. He died in 1715.

18. The palace and the gardens at Versailles, which he had built,[3] cost 500,000,000 francs.

19. How many dollars is his house worth?

20. It was formerly worth more than $25,000, but I don't know its value now.

B. Yesterday was Dec. 24. We were very busy all day, for we had not bought all our presents. Two weeks earlier we had sent those which were [4] to go to the United States. But we wanted to get [5] something for the lady at whose pension we are living, and for several other Parisians whose acquaintance we have made. Although the French celebrate New Year's Day more than we, and [6] Christmas is not so important, except among the children, still when I was in Paris a few years ago my French friends and I gave one another presents on [7] Christmas day. And I shall give them some to-day. So [8] we spent several hours yesterday in the stores. The decorations make them very pretty.

I said that Christmas was not important. That is not altogether true, for in the churches, of course, it is observed with great [9] solemnity. Although we were very tired, after having [10] spent so many hours in the stores and on [2] the streets, last night we attended the midnight mass. All the churches celebrate it the night before Christmas. We knew there would be a great many people in all the churches; as we wished to attend the service at the Church of the Madeleine, the one to which so many rich people go, we started early. At half-past ten we had already taken our places in the church and we were waiting for [11] the mass to begin. Hundreds of people came so late that they couldn't find any room. The mass was very beautiful. Afterwards we went out and took a walk on the boulevards. There we found great crowds, eating [12] and drinking [12] at the restaurants along the sidewalks; they were celebrating Christmas eve. We stayed there until after two o'clock in [13] the morning, then we came home and went to bed.

C. For several days now the principal streets have been very gay; for along the sidewalks there are booths where are sold toys, dolls, decorations for Christmas trees, and many other things. Flowers are sold also in the streets, more than in America; for the weather is much milder here in winter than in most of our American cities. I always like the crowds that fill the streets at [2] this season; every one is so happy, especially the little children. Everywhere you see them,[14] — on the sidewalks, in front of these booths, which I have just mentioned, and especially in the stores, which, like those where we trade in America, are all decorated to please [15] the children.

One might talk for hours or write whole volumes about the things that are seen in these great stores, which are quite as fine as those in [13] our American cities. All the best known people of the fairy tales are found here, — Cinderella, Tom Thumb, and many others who are favorites with [13] French children.

Let's say a word in passing about the beautiful mangers which are seen in the churches and in the store windows. It seems to me that often in America, we do not use symbolism enough to teach the children the story of Christ's birth. Here, in a little stable, are the Virgin, St. Joseph, with the child Jesus, often the Wise Men or perhaps the shepherds, and the cattle standing all around. We hang stars over the altars of our churches. Why not do [10] more, represent [10] the whole beautiful story of what happened at Bethlehem on that first Christmas day, more than 1900 years ago? It is better, it seems to me, to emphasize the religious side than to let [16] the children forget that it is especially a religious festival. They say that religion is dying out [7] in France. I do not believe it;

as long as one sees these representations of the manger at [13] Bethlehem, I shall continue to [13] believe that there is a basis of religious feeling in the French, in spite of all that people say to the contrary.

1. canal of Panama. 2. *dans*. 3. *faire* + inf. 4. *devaient*. 5. buy. 6. *que* + subj.; why? 7. omit. 8. *aussi;* with inverted order. 9. much. 10. inf. 11. *que* + imp. subj. 12. who were ... 13. *de*. 14. partitive. 15. *plaire* takes an ind. obj. 16. use *permettre* with subj.

EXERCISE XIII

STREET SCENES (Pages 91-95)

Grammatical study: numerals (continued); impersonal verbs; *pleuvoir, falloir*.

A. 1. It has been raining for three days. We shall have to stay in the house.

2. I am afraid it will rain [1] again to-morrow, — the fourth day of bad weather.

3. She has been here a week, and it has been bad weather every day.

4. It was raining when she came.

5. The first day it snowed; the second day it was windy.

6. The third day, although it didn't rain,[2] it was not pleasant.

7. She is hoping that it will be pleasant to-morrow, which will be the eighth day of her visit.

FRENCH COMPOSITION

8. It is ten o'clock; at one-thirty in³ the afternoon, they will start.

9. They have to travel ten hours; it will be dark when they arrive.

10. It was cold at seven o'clock this morning; it is not very warm now.

11. I must make a⁴ fire; in half an hour it will be warm enough.

12. It may rain to-morrow.

13. If it should rain, we should have to give up⁵ our trip to the country; let us hope it won't rain.

14. It is dark at 4.30 in³ the afternoon on the 21st of December.

15. That's the shortest day of the year, and we have to have lamps before four o'clock.

16. They had to go away on February 16.

17. They wanted to be here on the 22d, but as they had to be at home on the 21st, they started.

18. It had been snowing for eleven hours when they started, and it was very cold.

19. They needed warm clothing and thick shoes.

20. He was afraid⁶ he would have⁷ to start at eight o'clock, and that it would be raining⁷ when he arrived⁸ in the city.

B. In order to understand well the life of the French, one must see them eating⁹ and drinking⁹ on the sidewalks in front of the restaurants. Even in summer, it seems rather strange to³ see the chairs and tables on the sidewalks; but when it is warm, it is quite pleasant to³ eat there. But now it is cold, for winter has come. Those who eat there now have to wrap their mufflers tightly around their necks, to [10] protect themselves from [11] the cold wind which penetrates even the thickest clothing. There are two or three braziers, doing [12] their best [13] to [10] warm the people sitting [12] there, but it takes [14] a big fire to [10] heat a whole wide street! In front of the braziers there are usually several workmen and perhaps some "Apaches"; that is [15] the name given in Paris slang to the "toughs" whom you see in the streets. This [16] makes [17] the scene very picturesque.

In returning home from the theater this afternoon, we had to cross an old quarter of the city, where the streets are very narrow. We found there many things which attracted our attention. Even here, where there is hardly [18] room to walk, what one has to sell is put on the sidewalks in front of the stores, as in the other parts of the city. The streets are full of carts, where vendors have all sorts of things to sell, — fruit, fish, meat, vegetables, clothing, and so forth. Each trade has its peculiar cry or song, which is heard at all hours of the day. Some of these songs are quite picturesque, but one has to be very skillful to be able to understand what the people say.

C. Those who visit Paris see in the streets many things which seem strange to them at first. The costumes which are worn by some of the people they meet, the advertising posts, the stores, the street cars, and the omnibuses, even the houses, — everything is different enough to attract the attention of one who notices carefully what he finds in his walks. If one wishes to know

Paris thoroughly, he must take into account all that there is to see and to hear on the boulevards, in the streets, especially in the narrow streets of the old quarters of the city, even in the blind alleys, of which there are so many in Paris.

This morning we met a group of schoolboys, as we were walking out towards[19] Boulevard St. Michel. It was raining, but the weather made little difference to them; they were having a good time in spite of the rain. It was cold, too, and this[16] made[17] them even more lively than usual. All were carrying their portfolios, full of books and papers, slung over their shoulders.

All of a sudden there was heard[20] a noise, *pah-poum, pah-poum*. I wondered what it was. I had never heard such a noise since I had been[21] in Paris. So I asked[22] a student who was standing beside me on[22] the edge of the sidewalk, if he could tell me what was causing such a frightful noise. "Why,[23] yes," he said, "that's the firemen. Haven't you ever seen any?" He was right; they were coming up the street. It was the horns on the automobiles which were making that great noise. I was so interested in[22] what I saw that I followed them, which[24] I was able to do without any difficulty, for they were not going very fast. There's no need of hurrying; there's never any big fire here, as the houses are not made of wood. The fire was in the same street where I was walking; it was only a chimney fire,[25] and they put it out in a few minutes. I am told that here the owner has to pay the expenses when he calls out[26] the firemen — which[27] makes him more careful. If the house is insured, the insurance company pays them, but in any case the government pays nothing; it only gives the firemen a house and a small wage. Don't you think [28] that is [26] a good idea?

1. *je crains* + pres. subj., with *ne*. 2. imp. subj. 3. *de*. 4. partitive. 5. *renoncer à*. 6. *craignait* or *a craint*. 7. imp. subj., with *ne*. 8. cond.; why? 9. inf. 10. *pour*. 11. *contre*. 12. rel. clause. 13. *de leur mieux*, or *leur possible*. 14. *falloir*. 15. *voilà*. 16. *cela*. 17. *rendre*. 18. insert *enough*. 19. *du côté de*. 20. use *se faire entendre*, with impersonal subject. 21. imp. 22. *à*. 23. *mais*. 24. *ce que*. 25. fire in the chimney. 26. omit. 27. *ce qui*. 28. *trouver*.

EXERCISE XIV

THE WEATHER. HOW TO MAKE A FIRE (Pages 96–100)

Grammatical study: modal auxiliaries; uses of *devoir; devoir, craindre*, and verbs similarly conjugated.

A. 1. You must be tired. You ought not to have taken such a long [1] walk.

2. Remember that you are to go to the theater this evening.

3. He is complaining of what you have just done to him.

4. You must have hurt him. You ought to be more careful.

5. He was afraid the fire would go out.[2]

6. He is to be pitied,[3] for although he has been trying [4] for an hour to heat his room, he has not yet succeeded.

7. If she should complain [5] to the owner of the house,[6] would you join her [7] in what she said? [8]

8. You ought to.[9] Join us.[7]

9. You owe much to the one who brought you here.

10. You ought to be very grateful to him.

11. He was afraid you had forgotten [10] him.

12. We were to start at quarter of four, but we were afraid it would snow [2] and we have stayed in the house.

13. Tell him you pity him and that you will help him when you can.[11]

14. One ought to help all who suffer.

15. The artist had been painting for hours.

16. He must have been cold, for his fire had gone out long ago.

17. You should not have done that. If she had hurt herself, she would have complained to your father.

18. You should not do such things.

19. You will have to tell her what has happened. Why don't you tell her [12] now?

20. Do not put it off. Tell her she must be brave.

B. Winter in Paris is not the most agreeable season of the year. It is not cold, but it is very damp, and the sky is overcast most of the time, and it rains often. They say that once in a while, but very rarely, the Seine freezes over, but ordinarily one sees very little ice during the whole winter. It snows from time to time, but there falls only a very little snow, not enough so that one can [13] go sleighing. A few days ago when we got up, the thermometer registered eight degrees below zero, — which means Centigrade, of course; for they use the Centigrade system here. The sun was shining, the air was dry, and we [14] Americans thought [15] it was fine weather. But the Frenchmen with whom we talked that day all complained of the extreme cold. They kept saying [16] that they should die if it wasn't warmer before long.[17] They all wore mufflers or scarfs tightly wound around their necks, and some had even covered the lower part of their face, fearing that a little cold air might get [2] into their mouth or nose.

But it is no wonder that the French cannot [13] stand cold weather. Most of the houses are heated only by open fires, and they are not so warm as those to which we are accustomed. These people who complain when it is a little cold ought to spend a winter in the northern part of the United States or in Canada, where it is really cold, and where snow falls [18] almost every day from November until spring. They should go there in order to know what cold weather is. If they should do [5] that, what would they think of the weather of which they are complaining now?

C. A few days ago I called on your friend B., whom you introduced to me last summer. It was warm when we met him in September, and he told us that he thought the Paris weather was perfect. But now he is talking in [19] quite a different manner. When I went into his room he was trying to make a [20] fire burn; he had got down on his knees, and without knowing that I was there, he was talking to himself and complaining about this awful weather. You know how he dresses usually in winter. He wears only very thin clothing, and when everybody else is shivering and freezing, *he* says it is warm! You should see him now! He had his chair close to the fireplace, and when he had sat down he put his feet on another chair, so as to keep them above the floor! A great deal of air comes in [21] through the cracks around the windows. For you must remember that in most French houses the windows are really doors, which open onto the balcony. He had put pads in the cracks, to keep the air from coming in, but in spite of that the floor was cold, and he told me his feet were cold [22] as long as he was in his room. Poor fellow! how I pity him! I live this winter in one of the few houses which have a central heating system, so that my room is always warm.

I told B. that he didn't know how to make a [20] fire. He replied that I was not telling him anything new. "If there's one thing of which I'm absolutely sure," he said, "it is that I don't know how to make a fire which will really heat [13] the room. Show me what I need to do." But land! what do I know about that! I had not said that I knew more [23] about it than he. I had to do [24] my best, however. So we put on wood, coal, and briquettes, then we lighted the fire. It burns a few minutes, then it goes out. Well, several times we try, and finally behold! a real fire, which burns as if it were really to give a little heat. It doesn't even smoke, as most fires do, that I make. Madame X. says one should always cover a fire well with ashes as soon as it is burning well, so as not to have [25] to put on so much coal and wood. Well, that may be an economical way of making a fire, but *I* prefer to use plenty of wood and be warm.

I remember how Madame used to be afraid that I would catch cold [2] because I always left the windows wide open every night. She used to tell me that the night air was very dangerous, that enough air came in [21] through the chimney to ventilate the room. "Look out for draughts," she would say.[11] But I would tell her I wasn't afraid of draughts, and each night I would open the windows even when it was cold. One night she thought she would [26] scare me, by [27] telling me that the great mirror which was over the hearth might break; if there was a little heat left [28] in the chimney, the cold air from the window might cause much damage by cooling the glass quickly. But never mind, I said; it was better to pay for a broken mirror than to die of bad air. Poor Madame! I ought not to make fun of her, she was so good to [29] me.

I forgot to add that the fire which I made, and which I have just mentioned, went out after a few minutes.

1. a so long. 2. imp. subj. with *ne*. 3. *à* with active inf. 4. subj.; what tense? 5. what tense after *if?* 6. omit *of the house*. 7. what construction when dir. obj. is a refl. pron.? 8. cond.; why? 9. insert *do it*. 10. plup. subj. with *ne*. 11. what tense? 12. it. 13. pres. subj. 14. *nous autres*. 15. *trouver*; omit *was*. 16. *dire sans cesse*. 17. *avant peu*. 18. impersonal: *there falls some snow*. 19. *de*. 20. some. 21. cf. note 18. 22. he had cold at the feet. 23. *plus long*. 24. *de mon mieux*. 25. pres. subj. of *falloir*. 26. omit *she would*; put *scare* in inf. 27. *en* with pres. part. 28. *to be left* = *rester*; impersonal. 29. *pour* or *envers*.

EXERCISE XV

ART AT PARIS (Pages 100–104)

Grammatical study: modal auxiliaries: uses of *devoir* (continued); *devoir, pouvoir, savoir, falloir, vouloir.*

A. 1. Do you want him to come and [1] see you this evening?

2. Yes; I want him to come and to bring his sister with him.

3. He ought to have come yesterday.

4. What did she mean?

5. She meant that while she was willing to stay, still she hoped that she would be able to go away without waiting for [1] us.

6. May I come in? Yes, come in and sit down in front of the fire.

7. Shall I close the window? You must be cold.

8. You should not have stayed outdoors so long.

9. Please tell me what you wish me to do.

10. If I don't know how to do what you wish, I shall have to study, and that takes time.[2]

11. They could have stayed until evening if they had wished, but they would not.

12. They may have had to go, but I doubt it.[3]

13. Can you speak French? Yes, a little.

14. I cannot pronounce it very well, and if one is to speak a language, he must know how to pronounce it.

15. You ought to spend much time in pronouncing [4] French.

16. If you would do that, you could soon learn the difficult sounds.

17. But it takes patience.

18. If he comes while I am at the doctor's, ask him if he is willing to wait for me.

19. If he has to go away, tell him I should like to have [1] him come back this evening.

20. What shall I tell him when he comes?

21. Tell him I cannot do what he wants.

22. I ought to have sent him a letter, but I couldn't write, for I have broken my arm.

23. Who is to sing at the concert?

24. The lady whom we heard last summer was to sing, but she has such a cold that she cannot.

25. I have not been able to find out who has taken her place.

B. What interested you most, of all that you have seen at the Louvre? — Oh, I can't say; there are so many beautiful things there that I cannot make a choice. — Do you prefer the paintings or the sculpture? — I like the Venus of Milo and a few other statues, but for the most part, I have been most interested in the paintings, especially the ones which are in the French rooms. — Do you remember Greuze's painting, *La Laitière?* — Yes, I remember it well. But the ones I remember best are some of Millet's and Troyon's masterpieces. Everything that these artists have painted is fine. — I should like to be able to spend many hours before their paintings in the

Chauchard collection. I know only very little about art. To be able to judge pictures well one has to study art many years. I have been able to put into it only a little time. — But like most travelers, you know what you like, although you cannot always tell why a certain picture seems better than another. — We must get copies of some of these paintings, — the ones we like best. If I could, — I mean if I had enough money, — I should like to have a great many; for there are hundreds which are worth having copies of.[5] — But since we have only a little money, let us choose a few. — All right. I shall make a list of the ones I wish to buy. We will buy them when we go out this afternoon. — You have not said anything about the foreign painters. You have spoken only of the French artists. — Oh, of course, when I make that list I shall take into consideration all the painters of the other schools, — the Italians, the Spaniards, the Flemish, and so on. But if I am to choose, I must say I prefer the French painters of the Barbizon school; that is, Millet, Troyon, and so on.

C. One who loves art might stay in Paris many years, and every day he might find something new, which would be worth studying.[6] We have been here six months, and although we frequent the museums, there still remain several well-known collections of paintings and [7] sculpture which we have not visited. We have only begun [8] to get an idea of all the art there is [9] in this great city. Before I came here,[10] whenever some one talked to me about the chances I was to have to study art, I thought only of the Louvre. Of course the Louvre contains some of the finest pictures that have [11] ever been painted. It is no doubt the finest museum in the world. It is full of so many beautiful things that no one can know them all. After spending [12] several hours there, two or three times a [13] week, I have succeeded in choosing [4] a few pictures which I love more than all the others, — which I should like to have in my house, if I could! When I go there now there are certain rooms that I only pass through [14]; I have looked at all the pictures that they contain. I go directly to my favorite paintings, those that I have chosen, before which I want to stay as long as I can.

But paintings are only a part of what Paris offers us in the way of [15] art. There are numerous collections of old furniture, carriages, dishes, tapestries, jewels, enamels, and so on, which are well worth visiting.[16] Then for those who want to know how to understand the beautiful buildings that they see everywhere, there is the museum of the Trocadero, where are found models of all the most beautiful cathedrals. After being [12] in Paris a few weeks, everybody is interested in [17] architecture, — even those who do not know anything about it.

The government buys each year some of the best paintings which are shown at [18] the expositions. These, for the most part, are found at [18] the Petit Palais and at [18] the Luxemburg Museum. One who is studying art must take notice of these museums.

Paris can be seen in a week. That may be time enough for some of the travelers who come here. They go through the city as if there were nothing more interesting to see than the street cars and the signs. There are people who have to be satisfied with a week, although a year is hardly enough for them. For they know that one who has not studied thoroughly some of the masterpieces of art has really seen nothing. He may have lived in a foreign city; but he might as well have stayed at home.

1. omit. 2. it takes time for that. 3. of it. 4. *à* with inf. 5. which merit that we have copies of them. 6. *mériter + to be studied*, or *that one study it*. 7. repeat *de*. 8. *nous n'avons fait que commencer*. 9. all that there is of art. 10. *avant de* with inf. 11. subj. 12. perf. inf. 13. *par*. 14. cf. note 8. 15. *in the way of = de*. 16. cf. note 6. 17. *à*. 18. *dans*.

EXERCISE XVI

EDUCATION IN FRANCE (Pages 107–118)

Grammatical study: modal auxiliaries (continued); *connaître* and *savoir* and their uses.

A. 1. Who is that gentleman? He must be an artist.

2. Do you know him? No, I do not know him.

3. I know his name, but I have never been introduced to him.

4. May I come in? There is something important I wish to tell you.

5. You do not know what it is.

6. I know you could never guess what I am going to tell you.

7. He used to know them very well, but since they went away from this city he doesn't even know where they live.

8. How am I to know how many people will be here to-night?

9. I cannot tell you now. They will let you know [1] as soon as they arrive.

10. He wants you to know all those whom he has invited.

11. He says if you knew [2] them, you would like them.

12. They are to be here before eight o'clock.

13. When he has learned the rules for the agreement of past participles, he will know how to write French better.

14. I want you to know what he has done.

15. He ought never to have done it.

16. I knew at once what he had done, as soon as I found out [3] that he had gone away.

17. When you know them you will find them very pleasant people.

18. Before I knew [4] them I imagined [5] them to be [6] proud, but now I know they are not.

19. How long has your father known those ladies?

20. I do not know, but he has known them many years.

21. They must have been the first people he knew when he came to this city.

22. He does not know whether he can come to-night.

23. It may be that he will have to arrive a little late, but he will come before nine o'clock if it is possible.

B. I have just been reading a description of the system of education in France. It is an interesting subject, although a little bit[6] complicated. — Do you understand it? — Yes, pretty well. Most of what I have read is clear, but there are a few things which I do not understand, and I should like to ask [7] you a few questions. — Very well, ask [7] them.[8] I do not know whether I shall be

FRENCH COMPOSITION

able to answer [9] them all, but I will do my best. — All right. In the first place, do boys and girls study together in the French schools? — No, except in some small towns, where there are only a few pupils. — Then, do the children of the rich and those of the poor go to [10] the same school? — No, usually they don't,[11] and it is a pity. In a democracy, children of all classes ought to be together. — What is the difference between a *collège* and a *lycée?* — In the latter, there are more than a hundred pupils, and the state pays the expenses; in the former, there are less than a hundred, and the expenses are divided equally between the state and the city. — What do French children study? — My, that's a big question! In general, they study the subjects which are learned in our American schools, — mathematics, history, geography, ancient and modern languages, the sciences, and so on. As in America, some choose the "classical" education, while [12] others prefer the "modern." — Do they teach mechanic arts, carpentry, sewing, and so forth? — Oh yes, there are many special classes for the working people, in which these subjects are taught. And first aid to the injured, too; that is [13] a thing which we Americans ought to know more about. Those who have studied it in these municipal classes have an organization called "Les Secouristes français."

C. How am I to go about it [7] to get the names of pupils who are willing to correspond with American pupils? A friend of mine, a teacher in a public school, is anxious to have such a list, and she has asked me to get her one. But I do not know what to do. — It is not difficult. I remember what I did a few years ago, when I was looking for such a list. After visiting several schools where there were no such pupils, I found one at last where they were very glad to make such [14] an arrangement as I was asking. I had to address the rector of the University; for this school is under the direction of the University of Paris. He wrote me in reply that he was willing that the principal of the school should give me what I wished. The latter sent me to the censor, a man whose duties and powers we can hardly understand. The censor gave me the names of two teachers, to whom I wrote. Finally I received a list from one [15] of these teachers. It took a good deal of time to accomplish [16] my object, but I have always been grateful to the one who had asked me to do this for him, for without that I should never have been able to find out what I know about French schools. And I was glad also to meet so many French teachers. — You have just mentioned the University of Paris. There are other good universities, are there not? Oh yes, there are fourteen outside of Paris; they are all good. All are under the direction of the minister of public instruction, so that there is no great difference in the instruction given by the various universities. There are some which offer good summer courses, which are taken [17] by many American teachers and other people who are interested in the French language and literature. — What is the difference between the "free courses" and the "closed courses"? — The former may be taken by all who wish [18]; there are some of these lectures that are taken [17] by a great many people. The latter are reserved for those who are more serious and more advanced; those who take them hope usually to receive a degree. Although instruction is free in all courses, those who aspire to [19] the doctor's degree have to pay for [6] the examinations, and they have to have their theses printed, which costs considerable.[20] The doctor's degree from any French university is worth a great deal. — There are a lot of special schools. What is the "colonial school"? — There they teach what is needed [21] to [22] enter the colonial service; for France has a large colonial empire and it takes a great many men to govern it. And while [12] in America politics decides too often who shall have a certain position, France recognizes that those who are to be in charge of such difficult work [23] need special instruction.

1. *ils vous le feront savoir.* 2. what tense after *if?* 3. past anterior of *savoir.* 4. *avant de* with inf. 5. insert refl. ind. obj. 6. omit. 7. *faire.* 8. add *moi.* 9. *répondre* takes ind. obj. 10. *dans.* 11. add *do it.* 12. *tandis que;* why not *pendant que?* 13. *voilà.* 14. put *tel* immediately before *que.* 15. *l'un.* 16. come to. 17. *suivre;* use active, with inverted order. 18. use active. 19. hope to obtain. 20. a considerable sum (of money). 21. it is necessary to know. 22. *pour.* 23. plural.

EXERCISE XVII

THE CARNIVAL (Pages 118-121)

Grammatical study: *faire, laisser, voir,* and *entendre* with dependent infinitives; *faire, voir, suivre.*

A. 1. Have him come this evening at seven o'clock.
2. We shall be glad to see him and to hear him sing.

3. Have him bring some music.

4. Have him do it at once.

5. Do not let him put it off till [1] to-morrow.

6. He ought to be made to do his work without being told [2] each time.

7. Have you ever heard her sing? She sings this song beautifully.

8. We will have her sing it this evening when she comes.

9. Do not let me forget it.

10. Have him follow those whom he sees at the door.

11. Do not let them escape. If they should escape, I should never have anything [3] done by that man.

12. They have had tickets bought for them.

13. They wish to see Hernani played.

14. They have never seen this actor play.

15. If they should see him play, I am sure they would like him.

16. That man has been following us for an hour. Make him stop.

17. We don't let people [4] follow us if we can help it. Call that policeman, and he will follow the fellow.

18. She is having some new dresses made by the lady whom she introduced to you yesterday.

19. She has her make all her dresses.

20. When you see us coming, have them sit down.

21. That woman ought to make her children keep quiet.

22. She ought not to let them make so much noise.

23. I have heard it said that, although our army has been pursuing theirs for a long time, most soldiers think the enemy will be pursuing our men before long.[5]

24. Of what is he thinking? He ought not to let them do what they want to do.

25. If he should make them do their duty, everybody would be grateful to him for [6] it.

B. I have been waiting impatiently for a long time for the Carnival. I have heard so much said about it. They say the Frenchmen make the most of this day, for they know that several weeks of penitence and sober life will follow the single day of folly. However that may be, they certainly have a good time, and the police let them do as they please all day. In the evening, especially, everybody [7] you meet seems to be thinking only of amusing [8] himself. This afternoon, as we were coming out of the theater, a procession of students was commencing to form. Some of [9] them had strange costumes, and some had disguised themselves completely, but most of them had on their ordinary clothes; for this part of the fun is nothing in comparison with what follows, in the evening, when these students will all, no doubt, go to the masked balls, which take place everywhere in the city. We followed the procession which I mentioned as far as the Boulevard Sebastopol. But as we didn't wish to go any farther, we left it there. For a long time, however, we saw those fellows walking in the middle of the street. After leaving them we went to [10] a restaurant. While we were eating our dinner on the sidewalk, thousands of people passed us. We saw them throw confetti [11]; we heard them singing their songs; from time to time we saw some fellow, a little bolder than the others, embrace some pretty girl whom he met by chance. He didn't know her;

but never mind; that's part of the fun of the Carnival. And she permits it, without saying anything.[3] They made us cover our cups with our saucers; for if we had let them, they would have thrown confetti into the coffee. I do not like coffee that is full of confetti, part of which has been picked up [12] from the ground [13] by children, who are amusing themselves as much as their elders are.

C. We went to bed early last night, because we knew that to-day we should get up early and be busy all day. For to-day is [14] the Carnival. There isn't much to see in the morning, but soon after luncheon you would have thought [15] everybody had gone crazy. Everywhere we went we heard shouting and singing, and saw crowds of people walking in the middle of the street. It is especially on the boulevards of the left bank that you see the crowds amuse themselves. They do not let carriages of any [16] sort on them [17] during the hours when the crowds are there. Those who come and go [18] need all the room, not only on the sidewalks, but in the street as well. I had never seen so many people; there were thousands of them. All were pursuing the same idea, — to [6] amuse themselves as much as possible. Each one was thinking only of himself; or rather, we might say that each was thinking of all whom he met, but only to [19] make [20] life miserable for them for the moment. They in their turn would pay what they owed by [21] throwing confetti in [1] the eyes of all whom they saw. I never saw so much confetti used. The street was full of it.

After eating [22] our dinner at a restaurant without leaving the boulevards, we continued our walk. We hadn't

FRENCH COMPOSITION 59

wished to go home for dinner, because it takes at least an hour to eat it there; here we did not miss anything. If we had gone home, something might have happened here in which we should have been interested. So we stayed [23] where we could see what was being done. In the evening, it seemed as if [24] there were more people in the streets than before, although the rich had gone to their masquerade balls, or perhaps [25] to the theaters. But there are many poor people in Paris, who cannot afford such amusements, and who have to find their amusement in the streets. My friend and I stayed on the boulevards until after midnight [26]; nobody was thinking of going home then, — except us. After spending [22] the whole day on the streets, we were so tired that if we had had to stay there another hour, we should have fallen right [27] where we were. And that would have been a tragic ending for the Carnival. We took an auto bus, but still we did not get home until [28] after two o'clock. Even after going [22] to bed we heard people [29] singing and shouting in the streets, beneath our windows.

1. *à*.   2. *without one tell* (subj.) *it to him*.   3. *rien*, before inf.   4. use *on*.   5. *peu*.   6. *de*.   7. all those.   8. inf. 9. *d'entre*.   10. *dans*.   11. *confetti* (Italian) is itself plural. 12. change to active construction.   13. *par terre*.   14. it is to-day.   15. *dire*.   16. *aucune*.   17. enter there.   18. French says *go and come*.   19. *pour*.   20. *rendre;* why not *faire?* 21. *en*.   22. what part of the verb?   23. insert *there*.   24. *as if* = *que;* use subj.   25. *bien*.   26. until midnight past. 27. there.   28. not until = only.   29. omit.

EXERCISE XVIII

VERSAILLES, ST. DENIS, AND CHARTRES (Pages 126-131)

Grammatical study: subjunctive after expressions of desiring, avoiding, commanding, forbidding, consenting; *plaire*, *boire*.

A. 1. He does not want us to drink any coffee; he prefers that we should take milk.

2. What you have just done will please your mother; she never wanted you to go away.

3. The man will order them to come at once; he is anxious that they should start before six o'clock.

4. I long to see them; when they come, tell them not to go away without visiting me.

5. He has broken his arm; the doctor forbids his going out.

6. He used to drink coffee, but for six months the doctor has not permitted him to drink it.

7. We are anxious that you should please those who used to make you so happy.

8. Tell her to start when she wishes to.

9. The rain prevented his coming; he wanted to come, but couldn't.

10. The mayor ordered all the streets to be cleaned.

11. The doctor wants him to drink only water.

12. Have that young man come in, if you please; I want him to tell me what he was doing.

13. The judge ordered them to have the man punished.

14. Do you want us to drink the milk that you gave us?

15. He hoped what he had done would please her.

FRENCH COMPOSITION

16. Do not prevent his doing that; let him do it.

17. She wanted you to please the lady who came in a few minutes ago.

18. Please tell them not to go away before eight o'clock.

19. If you should drink what he has just given you, it would keep you from sleeping.

20. As soon as you wake up, have the servant bring in the breakfast.

21. He wants to avoid her meeting that man, if he can.

22. If your voice should please him, he would, no doubt, wish you to sing again.

23. We were anxious that he should begin what he had to do.

24. Your father is going to order the young man to pay what he owes.

25. Do you want him to tell you the names of those who have come?

B. Is St. Denis worth visiting [1]? — Certainly, it is a pretty little town, and it is always worth while to observe life in these French towns. What makes it important is [2] that it contains the tombs of most of the kings and queens. Under the church are buried Louis XVI and Marie-Antoinette, the ones who were ruling at the beginning of the Revolution, and others. — What is there to see at Chartres? — Why, what a question! Don't you remember the beautiful church with [3] its [4] superb stained-glass windows? I have spoken to you about it many times. All who love Gothic architecture love that church. I want you to see that town before leaving France. — We have not gone to Versailles, either.[5] I should like to have you tell me something about the historical events which have taken place there. Tell me, please, what is meant by this "tennis court." What took place there? — That is where [6] the representatives of the people, or of the "third estate," to use the French term, assembled in 1789 and took [7] an oath not to separate before giving their country a constitution. The tennis court is not far from the palace, where they had been refused [8] admittance.[9] The building serves as a [10] museum now. — How do you get to Versailles from Paris? — There are trains which leave the North Station or the Quai d'Orsay Station. One can go by street car if one prefers that way of traveling, but it takes more time to go that way,[11] of course. I shall always remember one very pleasant trip which I took [7] to Versailles a few years ago. We went by [12] boat to Meudon, down the Seine, and from there we went through the woods to [13] Versailles. It was in the [12] autumn; the heather, which I think [14] is very pretty, and the red and yellow leaves made the woods very beautiful. We enjoyed that little walk; naturally the park at Versailles was most charming at [15] that season. — Can't we take that same walk some [16] day when we have nothing else to do? — Certainly; shall [17] we not do it to-morrow? If it is pleasant, we will get up early, and I know that way of spending the day will please you.

C. Well, here we are at Versailles. Let us go to the palace at once. There are many things to see in the palace. Most of the paintings are not worth much, but there are some that are interesting because they show us various historical events. — What is it that I see to the right of the entrance gate? Is it a chapel? — Yes, it is a very beautiful chapel, although I think Gothic architecture is better for churches than that of the Renaissance. Remember that kings and queens used to live in this palace, and they had their own chapel. — How large this palace is! Can we ever see all that it contains, in a single afternoon? — No, we shall go through most of the halls quickly, for it seems to me it is not worth while to spend much time in [18] examining all there is to see. We shall go to the Gallery of the Mirrors, where in 1871 William I, king of Prussia, had himself made emperor of Germany. That was during the Franco-Prussian war, when the German army had been besieging Paris for several months. — How magnificent all these halls are! The balls and banquets which took place here in [18] the times of the great kings must have made these halls very gay. But when I think of all the money that this palace and the park cost, five hundred million francs, I do not wonder that the people rose [19] at last and [20] demanded [19] that they be given their rights. Those kings wanted the people to work for them and made them do whatever [21] they desired; they never thought of what they owed their subjects.

I think we have seen all we wish to here; let us go out now. I am anxious for you to see the Great Trianon and the Little Trianon. — What is a Trianon? — That is a name given to some little castles on the other side of the park; Louis XIV had the former built for Madame de Maintenon, while the latter, built by King Louis XV, belonged to Countess du Barry. I like [22] these better than the great palace. There are so many things to see in it that one feels confused after spending a half-hour there. But here there are only a few rooms and they are smaller; everything they contain is full of interest for those who have studied French history ever so little. Let us hurry; if we do not, we shall not be able to see the pond in the middle of the park, or the canal, as it is called. I want to show you the fountains, too; they are very famous. It is too bad they are not playing [23] to-day. We must come back some [16] day when we can see them all play. It is so expensive to have them play that they do so only a few times each [24] year now. — What is that, high up in the trees? — That is mistletoe; they say it hurts the trees, but I think [25] it makes them pretty. And see how they are all covered with ivy. Isn't that beautiful? I wish there were more ivy at home; it makes what it covers so beautiful. Although I do not like their cutting the hedges and the bushes in such [26] exact forms, I think [25] the trees are fine.[27]

1. a visit. 2. *c'est.* 3. *à* in descriptions. 4. the. 5. *non plus.* 6. it is there that. 7. *faire.* 8. change to active. 9. to admit them. 10. *as a = de.* 11. *ainsi.* 12. *en;* no article. 13. *jusqu'à.* 14. *trouver;* omit *is.* 15. *dans.* 16. *un;* trans. *when* by *où* or *que.* 17. *pourquoi ne pas le faire,* or *ne voulez-vous pas* + subj. 18. *à.* 19. subj.; why? what tense? 20. repeat conj. 21. all that. 22. use *plaire.* 23. subj. 24. *par.* 25. *trouver.* 26. *so.* 27. use a superlative absolute: *tout ce qu'il y a de plus beau.*

EXERCISE XIX

SPRING IN PARIS (Pages 131-135)

Grammatical study: subjunctive after expressions of approval or disapproval, emotion, or sentiment; *vaincre*, *prendre*, and verbs similarly conjugated.

A. 1. I am sorry that she has broken her arm.

2. It is better that you should go away now; he doesn't wish you to stay any [1] longer.

3. We are glad that they understand what you have just said to them.

4. It is time for her to come; we want her to tell us what she is going to do.

5. He is glad that the French are conquering.

6. I was surprised that you should not understand that.

7. Have you taken what I left on the table for you? I am glad you can use it.

8. Take that book, and use it; we should like to have you keep it.

9. It is a pity that she cannot come; tell her we hope she will be better to-morrow.

10. We are afraid the enemy will conquer us.

11. If they should conquer, what would they do with [2] the vanquished?

12. Napoleon conquered the Italians; he didn't want them to oppose him.

13. As soon as he understood what we were going to do, he ordered us to go away.

14. It is better for you to take what he gives you.

15. I am glad he has learned French so well.

16. He is learning to speak it, but he is afraid he will not be able to understand it when he goes to France.

17. If he should go to Paris, would he understand what he heard [3]?

18. They complain that we have never arrived on time.

19. The soldier was not afraid they would conquer his country.

20. It is good that they got up so early this morning.

21. It is necessary for them to start early; they are afraid they will not arrive on time.[4]

22. Your father wanted you to take what was in your room.

23. What do you want me to take? I don't understand you.

24. She wants you to have some flowers sent to her.

25. I was glad that she had come.

B. Why are all the store windows full of fish? There are some of chocolate, and some of pastry, while there are quantities of post cards with pictures of fish. — It is because the first of April is the festival of fishes. Formerly French people used to send each other real fishes on [1] that day. — It was snowing a little when we got up this morning, but now the sun is shining. We might go into [5] the country this afternoon. At first I was afraid it might snow or rain, but now it is warm and fine. Let us take a street car and go to Fontenay-aux-Roses. — I should like very [1] much to walk through the fields. Shall we be able to find fields and woods near Paris? — Oh yes; in an hour we shall see some. After leaving the car we shall go out of the village, and in a few minutes we shall be in a place where we can hear birds and see many trees. I want you to hear some larks sing. — Oh, I should like to hear some. When I hear them sing, I shall recognize them at once, I am sure.[6] — They go up very high into the sky, so high that they can scarcely be seen; you only hear [7] the marvelous music which descends from the sky. I once heard one that sang more than three minutes without stopping. — Are there many larks near Paris? — There are thousands; the woods and fields are full of them. Everywhere you will hear them sing. Parisians even kill them to eat them; I have seen some in the stores. — What a pity! It is too bad that they should kill birds that give so much pleasure and which have inspired so many poets.

C. What I have said so many times about the weather, since I have been [3] here,[8] is not a description of spring at Paris. Those who visit this city in winter choose a bad season; I am afraid they think it is never pleasant here. Two of my friends came January 25 and they stayed with me until February 11; it rained nearly every day, and the sun shone only twice while they were here. They say it is very hot in summer, so that Paris is rather disagreeable then. But the spring and the fall are most delightful.[9] It is warm now every day, and what pleases me most, I have been getting along without a fire for more than two weeks. Every morning I put my chair on the balcony and read there; when I have letters to write, I write them there, too. I spend hardly any time in the house. Sometimes I take my books and go into the park, or to the Luxemburg garden.[10] I am glad the garden is so near the house, because I can go there in a very few minutes. But I find I can accomplish very little. It is in vain [11] for me to open my book. I read a page, then a bird begins to sing. I do not know the names of many French birds, but I have been studying our American birds so long that I can recognize these without any difficulty. After following a blackbird a few minutes and listening to [12] his ravishing song, I sit down again in vain [11] on my bench. I can't make myself study. The gardens and parks are full of blackbirds, and I love their song.

A few days ago my friend and I went into the country, where we spent a whole afternoon. The buds come out on the trees before the middle of April, and there are violets and other flowers in the fields, even during the last ten days of March. The chestnuts along the Champs-Elysées blossom toward the end of April.

The farmers who live near Paris raise many early vegetables for the markets of the city. We saw some when we were in [5] the country. The paths that we followed led us across fields where lettuce and asparagus were growing,[13] which are to be sold soon in the city. All whom we met in the fields were working, for there is much to do. Beside the path, we picked some violets and some little yellow flowers of which I did not know the name. I asked a farmer if he could tell it to me, and he told me they were called "boutons d'or." At first, I didn't understand what he meant, but after thinking a little, I said to myself that he was right; they were just [14] little buds, and they seemed to be of gold. The fields are covered with them.

1. omit. 2. *de.* 3. what tense? 4. *à temps.* 5. *à.*
6. of it. 7. the idiom is *faire* + inf.: *you only do* + *to hear.*
8. insert *it.* 9. use a superlative absolute construction: *all that there is of most.* . . . 10. garden of the Luxemburg.
11. in the idiom *avoir beau* the person is the subject of the verb *avoir*, the other verb is in the infinitive. 12. *écouter* takes dir. obj. 13. change the sentence so as to use an impersonal verb.
14. just = only.

EXERCISE XX

THE MARKETS (Pages 135–140)

Grammatical study: subjunctive after expressions of doubt, denial, etc., and after expressions of perceiving, thinking, knowing, etc.; *faillir, fuir.*

A. 1. He almost fell as he was approaching the house; I was afraid he would fall.

2. He doubts whether you can get any flowers at the market to-day.

3. Are you sure that the woman with [1] the broken arm fell [2] in the street?

4. It may be that the armies of our enemies are fleeing.

5. It seems to me that they must have come now.

6. We were not sure that they would come, but we hoped they would come.

7. That building with [1] the two towers must be the cathedral; do you think it's the cathedral?

8. I do not think it is the one they were speaking to us about.

9. Do you think it will be fine weather to-morrow?

10. They were failing when we came, but I think they will succeed now.

11. The newspapers do not deny that the armies have fled.

12. What are they buying? Are they sure that what they are buying is worth something?

13. They were fleeing, but I did not think they had been defeated.

14. Do you think that man with [1] the two books is right?

15. I think he is wrong, but I am not sure.

16. If I were sure that he was wrong, I should tell him so.

17. The general is afraid his men will fail.

18. If they should fail, he would be sorry that he had made them go.

19. If they should flee, would they succeed in [3] escaping the enemy? What do you think about it?

20. When they flee, where will they go? Are you sure they will go to the city?

21. It is too bad they have failed; I was hoping they would be able to succeed.

22. To whom shall I give these newspapers? Do you think your father wishes to read them?

23. He is anxious for you to give them to the people who need them most.

24. The generals order their men to flee if they fail in what they are trying to [4] do.

25. Those who were buying vegetables did not think the prices would be so high.

B. Sunday morning, after coming out of church, we

went to the bird market [5] which is on [6] the Ile de la Cité, quite near the cathedral. It is most interesting.[7] We saw a great [8] many birds. The ones that pleased us most were the nightingales; we had never seen any. Of course, those that are in this market, shut up in cages, do not sing, but we had heard people [8] speak of them so much that we were anxious to see some. It seemed as if there were thousands of people in [9] the square, some of whom were buying birds; but most of those that we saw were only walking through [10] the market and looking at the birds. It was in vain [11] for the vendors to talk to them; they couldn't make them buy anything. It was evident that these people, like us, had come there only to see what there was to see. One who intends to study French character must go to the markets; he sees so many people there, of all sorts.

There is a flower market [12] near the bird market; we went there after leaving the latter. It is better to visit these places on [8] Sunday, when there are more people there than on [8] the other days. Every time that I take a walk I buy some flowers, for they are so cheap, and one sees so many everywhere. Most of those that are being sold now come from quite near the city. There are quantities of violets, crocuses, anemones, tulips, lilacs. At the market Sunday there were a few lilies of the valley; I had not seen any in the streets.

But the real market which all those who want to see French life must visit is [13] the Central Market.[14] It may be that one can form an idea of French character without going there, but I doubt it. We have gone there several times about midnight, after leaving the theater, to see the vendors who have just arrived from the country with what they have to sell.

C. About ten o'clock in the morning, a few days ago, we arrived at the Central Market. We had been walking for an hour; it was beautiful weather, and we could never have stayed in the house. After walking a while we thought of the market; it seemed to me it must be a good day to visit it, for there would probably be many people there. We crossed through the sections where fish and meats are sold; in one place, where some live fish had escaped from the basket and had made [15] the floor all slippery, we came near falling, and breaking our arms. Then my friend was almost knocked over by a little cart, pushed by a boy who was hurrying without looking out for [16] those who might [2] be in his way. In spite of a few accidents, we succeeded in [3] reaching the section where vegetables were being sold. We took our places near an old woman who was discussing the price of her potatoes with a lady who evidently wanted to buy some, but who was not willing to pay for them [17] the price asked by the vendor. We listened to them a few minutes as they bargained. Their conversation was most interesting. At last they had told each other all they had to say about the price of those potatoes. When the bargain had been made, and the lady had gone off, carrying the potatoes, which she had bought quite cheap, we approached the old woman and spoke to her. "Have you been here long?" I asked her. "Heavens, yes," she said,[18] "I have been here for hours. Just think,[19] at seven o'clock

FRENCH COMPOSITION 73

last night we started for the city, my man and I. We live in a suburb [20] some twenty kilometers from here, and we have to start early in order to get here in time, before all the places are [21] taken. We arrived at the market about midnight. Already there were twenty or more [22] farmers. After putting ourselves in this good corner, we lay down on our carts and took [23] a good nap for a couple of hours." "But how could you sleep here where there is so much noise? There must be a great deal even at two o'clock in the morning, for the farmers are arriving at every moment. It seems to me I could never get to sleep here. And that cart can't [24] be the most comfortable bed in the world!" "Oh, sir, one gets used to it. After working hard all day, as we [25] farmers do, one can sleep anywhere." "But say! you do not mean that you worked all day on [6] the farm, before setting out for the city?" "Why,[26] yes, certainly; there is a lot to do, and there is nobody except [27] us to [28] do it. We have to work many hours each day; if we didn't, we should not have anything to sell." "Have you grown everything that you have to sell?" "Yes, sir, these potatoes, turnips, cabbages, and all the other vegetables that you see there, we have grown them all on [6] our little farm." Then a lady approached her to [28] buy something; and after thanking her for [4] what she had told us, and giving her a little tip, we went away to buy some bananas and some grapes of a [29] man whose cart was on [4] the other side of the market.

1. what preposition in descriptions? 2. what tense? 3. *à* with inf. 4. *de*. 5. *marché aux oiseaux*. 6. *dans*. 7. use a superlative absolute construction. 8. omit. 9. *sur*. 10. cf.

note 7, Ex. XIX. 11. cf. note 11, Ex. XIX. 12. cf. note 5.
13. *ce sont*. 14. *Halles Centrales*. 15. what verb for *make*
when followed by a noun and a predicate adjective? 16. *avoir
soin de*. 17. dir. obj. 18. inverted order; why? 19. *se
figurer*; omit *just*. 20. at. 21. subj. 22. *une vingtaine*.
23. *faire*. 24. *devoir*. 25. insert *autres*; why? 26. but.
27. nobody except = only. 28. *pour*. 29. *à*.

EXERCISE XXI

FONTAINEBLEAU (Pages 140–143)

Grammatical study: subjunctive in adjectival clauses, — clauses
of characteristic, after a superlative, with "whoever," "whatever," etc.; *rire*, *vêtir*.

A. 1. These are the most beautiful churches that we have ever seen.

2. Whatever they may think of that, they ought to dress their children better.

3. Is there no one here who knows how to do what I want done [1]?

4. They were all laughing at [2] the story he had just told; it was the best one they had ever heard.

5. Whatever you do, do not laugh when he comes in.

6. Is there any one who knows who those people dressed in black are [3]?

7. He used to dress his children as well as possible.

8. He didn't want others to dress their children better than his.

9. We did not want you to laugh; we were afraid you would destroy the effect of what we were saying.

FRENCH COMPOSITION

10. He is looking for some one who can take him to the doctor's; he has broken his arm.

11. He [4] who laughs last, laughs best.

12. The finest pictures that man has ever painted are being sold cheap.

13. She will clothe her daughter in a manner which shall please all whom she meets.[5]

14. I have never seen any picture which is worth more than this one.

15. A little girl dressed all in white is at the door; she wishes to find some one who will help her.

16. The only time she has fallen was when it was snowing a few days ago.

17. Whatever books you read, do not forget the ones your father recommended to you.

18. If there were any one here who could do that, I should be glad.

19. I am surprised that you should laugh at [2] such a thing.

20. Whatever we have said to him, he has never even smiled.

21. I am sorry he is sick; do you think he will die?

22. Is there nothing which can make you happy?

23. They dressed [6] quickly, because they were afraid their friend would come early.

24. What do you want him to send you?

25. Whatever he sends me, I hope it will be something that I can use.

B. I am glad that it is such a fine day. For to enjoy Fontainebleau one must have [7] good weather. There are so many things to see, and we must see as much as possible of the forest. — You have talked so much about this place that I long [8] to see what there is that is [9] so wonderful. But whatever there may be here, however beautiful the palace and the forest may be, I am sure that I shall enjoy all that I see [5] to-day. One would have to be very stupid not to [10] enjoy a day in the country when it is so beautiful. — There is the castle in front of us. It is to my mind the most interesting castle that one can visit. It contains so many things which serve to make history more clear and real. Let us go in right away. — What fine tapestries! And what beautiful furniture! There is nothing which pleases me more than a fine collection, like this one, of old furniture. How many curious things [11] there are in these rooms! — There is the cradle of the "King of Rome." — Who was this "King of Rome;" of whom you speak? I have heard you speak of him several times. — He was the son of the great Napoleon. After Napoleon had been defeated and sent to St. Helena, this little son was kept a prisoner in Austria; he was very weak and died after a few years. He never had enough strength either [12] of body or [12] of character, to oppose those who had united to conquer his father. — What does that *N* mean, which I see on all these chairs, embroidered in gold? — Don't you understand that? It serves to explain to us that everything showing this letter belonged formerly to Napoleon. Look at this manuscript. It is Napoleon's abdication. His writing is not very legible. You can hardly read it. But here is a translation of it.

C. After spending several hours in the castle,[13] looking at the marvelous collection of old furniture which it contains, we came out into the gardens. There we amused ourselves a few minutes by [13] feeding the famous carp, of which the ponds are full. But soon we set out for the forest. On the way we passed through the charming village, the prettiest and cleanest that I have ever seen in France. In [14] the square near the castle, is a monument in memory of Rosa Bonheur, who used to paint here; her paintings of animals are known to [2] everybody. Remember, also, that near here is the town of Barbison, where the artists of the so-called Barbison school [15] did a great part of their work.

The forest of Fontainebleau covers a vast territory. The government owns it and keeps it up. As in all forests in [2] Europe, everything that is possible is done to avoid a fire's starting. All the little bushes which are of no use [16] and all the dead branches are destroyed; they cut off the lower branches of the pine trees, which only detract from their beauty. Before coming to Europe I had imagined that all the care [17] they took [18] to prevent fires must make the forests less beautiful than those that we love so much. In them [19] the ground is always covered with dead branches, and there are so many low bushes and everything is so wild that one can hardly walk there; it is very beautiful, but there is nothing which can prevent a fire's destroying a large part of it. The French certainly protect their forests well, and I must say that I think they have made them even more beautiful in protecting them against fires.

Through the whole forest there are excellent roads,

well kept up. The Touring Club of France, an organization to which all who go through these woods are grateful, puts up numerous sign boards, which make it [7] very easy to find one's way about.

High trees, deep ravines, great rocks, make [20] this forest a place of which any country might well be proud. I am sure if I could spend weeks here I should never become tired of roaming through the woods. Fontainebleau is indeed one of the places that every traveler ought to visit. Remember it, I beg of you,[21] when you go to France.

1. done = to have done, i.e. *faire faire*. 2. *de*. 3. put verb immediately after subject. 4. in proverbial expressions antecedent is usually omitted. 5. what tense? 6. *s'habiller*. 7. omit. 8. in the idiom *tarder de* there is an impersonal subject, while the person is the indirect object: *il me tarde de*. 9. that is = *de*. 10. *pour ne pas*. 11. order = *how there are (of) curious things*. 12. *ni . . . ni*. 13. *à* followed by inf. 14. *sur*. 15. *école dite de Barbison*. 16. serve for (*à*) nothing. 17. plural. 18. gave themselves. 19. the latter. 20. insert *of*. 21. I beg you of it.

EXERCISE XXII

MONT ST. MICHEL (Pages 144-146)

Grammatical study: subjunctive in adverbial clauses, — with conjunctions of time before which or up to which, conjunctions of purpose or result, condition, and concession, conjunctions of negative force, with *que* replacing other conjunctions; *taire, acquérir*.

A. 1. Keep quiet; although that may be true, I doubt it.

2. She has been sleeping for an hour; unless you keep quiet, she will wake up.

3. Open that door, so that your father may find it open when he comes.

4. Although the soldiers have been in this country six months, they have not yet conquered it.

5. Until they go away, you ought to do what you can to make their visit pleasant.

6. Please give him this before he goes away.

7. Although they have not gone away yet, they are to start soon.

8. In case he cannot stay, tell him we are sorry he has to go.

9. However poor one may be, he should always pay his debts.

10. If it does not snow or rain, we shall start to-morrow morning.

11. They came in without our seeing them.

12. Make him keep quiet; I am afraid he will wake your father.

13. He would keep quiet if you should order him to do so.

14. She set out early, for fear she might miss the train.

15. Are you afraid they will not get up in time?

16. She says she cannot do anything unless that child keeps quiet.

17. Although she got up early this morning and has been working hard, she is not tired.

18. Not that you will acquire anything worth while,[1] but try it.

19. He was acquiring bad habits without any one's knowing it.

20. He will acquire riches, provided he sets [2] to work.

21. Whether he acquire riches or remain poor, he will be happy.

22. Although you may be hungry, I do not want you to eat dinner until [3] I come back.

23. In case it rains, they will not go away.

24. However hard that lesson may be, learn it so that you can recite it well.

25. Although they have died, the country will remember them always.

B. Mont St. Michel, an island on the coast of Normandy, is one of the most interesting places that the traveler can visit. It is really an enormous rock, which rises out of St. Michael's Bay [4]; this is part of the English Channel. Formerly this rock was completely surrounded by water, but in 1879 a great dike, more than fifteen hundred meters long,[5] was built, which connects the rock with [6] the mainland; so that now it is really not an island. Mont St. Michel is the name of the rock, and of the town, as well, which is on it.

The glory of this place is the beautiful church, built for the most part in [6] the eleventh century. It is on the top of the rock, and can be seen from afar. St. Aubert founded the church in 708. St. Michael had come to him and had told him to do so. Good St. Aubert built only a little wooden church. But after a while the king began a magnificent stone church. In it one sees numerous hidden stairways in the middle of the walls, cells where prisoners were kept from time to time, little rooms which are reached through low, narrow, passage ways. In one of these rooms there is a great wheel which the prisoners used to turn to bring up their provisions. Some one would get inside and walk, and as the wheel turned it pulled up, by means of a cord, a car full of the various things they needed.

C. As long as I live, I shall remember the day we spent at Mont St. Michel. We had gone to bed, the night before, a little bit [7] discouraged and very tired, for to reach this place one has to take [8] a long, hard journey. Even after traveling all day, we had not yet reached our destination; we were only at Pontorson, a little village two or three kilometers away from [9] the place we had come to visit. So, when we went to bed about 9.30 that evening, we were wondering [10] whether we had not made a mistake in coming here. Although we had seen photographs of this strange rock with its church, and had read descriptions of it, we were afraid it was not worth all the trouble it takes to get there.

But we got up early the next morning, and after eating breakfast, went to the shore. The tide was high, the sun was shining on the water, and off there in the middle of the bay, there was the great rock, 165 feet high,[11] having at its foot houses which seemed to cling to it, and at the top a church, surmounted by [12] a steeple, which even from there we could recognize as [13] something marvelously beautiful. They say the view used to be even more beautiful before the dike was built. This dike makes the trip to the rock more comfortable, but it impairs the beauty of the place.

FRENCH COMPOSITION

Soon we were in the little town, and were walking in its street — for there is only one — which ends in [6] steps leading to the abbey. Of course we went first to the church. All that it contains is most interesting. After examining its nave and choir, the cloister and all the other parts of this wonderful building, we came out onto a platform to enjoy the view over [14] the bay, which is most [15] delightful.

After luncheon we went around the island, walking on the sand, which the tide, on going out, had left dry. The tide rises very quickly, and those who go around the island on foot must look out not to [16] get caught.

I must not forget the omelets and the cutlets, which have made the hotels of Mont St. Michel famous throughout all France.[17] All who come here eat some at "Widow Poulard's establishments," [18] — a name known to [12] all who have visited this town, although good widow Poulard herself has been dead for many years.

To end well [19] a perfect day, we went and sat down on the rocks about seven o'clock to watch the sunset and the incoming tide. Both these spectacles have a peculiar charm at [20] this place, and luckily we were able to see them at the same time.

1. which is worth. 2. *se mettre à*. 3. before. 4. *la baie St. Michel*. 5. long by (*de*) more . . . ; *de* = the Latin ablative of measure. 6. *à*. 7. omit. 8. *faire*. 9. at two or three kilometers from. 10. inverted order; why? 11. cf. note 5. 12. *de*. 13. *pour*. 14. *sur*. 15. of the most. 16. the idiom *to look out not to* = *to guard one's self from, se garder de*, + inf. 17. through (*par*) all France. 18. *widow Poulard* goes after *establishment*, without any connecting preposition, and without any article. 19. put *bien* before the infinitive. 20. *dans*.

EXERCISE XXIII

BRITTANY AND NORMANDY (Pages 147-155)

Grammatical study: subjunctive in principal clauses, review of subjunctives; tenses used after *si*, meaning "if"; tenses used after *quand* and similar conjunctions, pleonastic *ne* after comparatives; *vivre, cueillir*.

A. 1. When he picks his roses, he will send us some.

2. So long as he lives, he will never forget what you have just told him.

3. If he should pick those apples now, they would not be good to eat.

4. May he have the strength to [1] finish what he has so well begun!

5. He has been picking cherries for an hour.

6. Long live those who have made this possible!

7. Before they start may he be able to do more than he has done!

8. As soon as he has picked his fruit, I will tell him to come into the house.

9. She wants us to wait until she has picked a dozen roses.

10. Do not pick those flowers; they are not yours.

11. We thought she had killed herself, but she is alive.

12. That old man has been living many years, and says he never saw such a thing.

13. He was living at the time of [2] the Civil War.

14. We were glad he was living; we were afraid he had died.

15. Wait until [3] we have read these newspapers.

16. When she comes into the room, tell her that it is colder than she thought.

17. You have more books than your father has.

18. He wants you to have more money than he has been able to give you.

19. She is older than I had imagined her to be.[4]

20. She has picked more apples than I had seen on that tree.

21. As soon as he has lived ten years more,[5] he will be a hundred years old.

22. He has less courage than you had thought.

23. They must have eaten more cherries than you gave them.

24. If he is sick, let [6] me know.[7]

25. When you are ready, tell me,[7] so that I may pick some roses before I start.

B. I have been told many times that Brittany is more beautiful in [8] the spring than it is at [9] the other seasons. However that may be, I am sure that in [8] the month of April, when we spent a few days there, it was most charming. The fruit trees were all in blossom, there were a great many flowers everywhere, and the birds were singing; all Nature was alive again. Winter here is much less severe than it is in the American city where we have been living for several years. But in spite of that, after staying in the house the larger part of the time, we were glad to spend a few days in the country. After leaving Paris, we had gone into Normandy, and after staying a few days there had come to Brittany. We took some long walks through the fields and had a good time, for there are more things to see than I can describe. If I should talk to you for hours or should write whole books, I could not tell you [10] half of what we saw. Although we had been in France for several months, we had been in the country only two or three times. Hence, we avoided the cities so that we might study the life of the peasants. We wanted to see those who work on [9] the farms. Before coming here we had wondered whether we should be able to talk with them. We found some who couldn't understand French; for we must remember that the Bretons are Celts, who have their own Breton language. But whenever we found any who spoke French, they understood what we said, and we were able to understand them without any difficulty, which pleased us. Most of those we met were willing to answer our questions, and told us more things about their life than we could have learned if we had only read books.

C. Let us leave the city entirely to-day, and go into the country. — All right; I don't doubt we shall see many things of interest in this way. Where shall we go? — There is a little village [11] some ten kilometers from here, where we can get luncheon; let us go there. On the way, we shall see some farms; and as we shall walk, we can study the life of the peasants better than we could ever study it if we rode in an [4] automobile or a [4] carriage. — What [12] do they call those yellow flowers? — Furze. Aren't they pretty? — Yes, but their thorns are rather disagreeable. What a lot of them there are! The country is covered with them. The bushes are quite large. Are they used for anything [13] ? — Yes, the peasants use

them to make fires of them. You will see great piles of
them in some of the yards. — Why is that cross put [14]
at the side of the road? And there's another at that
crossroad. What do they signify? — This one shows
the place where some one was killed. They must all have
some meaning of that sort. The Bretons are very pious. —
Why! What is that bird? — That is a cuckoo. You
recognize its song, don't you? — Yes, but I had never
either seen or heard any before, except in the clocks. —
There is a peasant woman, taking care of the sheep. What
has she in [8] her hand? — It is her knitting; for these
people are very industrious; they never waste any time. —
What a picturesque house! Its roof is of thatch, isn't it?
— Yes, and notice that its walls are of white-washed stones.
Let's go in. We will buy a little milk, which will give us
a [10] chance to see the interior. — Why! the ground serves
as [1] a floor, and look at those great beams which make the
ceiling. What an enormous fireplace! They cook there,
don't they? — Yes, these peasants have no stove. —
There is a little chapel. I should like to go in. Is it permitted? — Certainly. You will see that it is most simple;
it has fewer decorations than those fine churches have
which you have seen in Paris and the other cities. The
pilgrimages that are made to some of these chapels, especially to those near the sea, are very interesting. I
wish we might see one. — What is that woman doing over
there? — She is doing the washing. She wets the clothes
in that little pond, then after spreading them on that rock,
beats them with that stick, or *battoir*, as it is called. —
Well, that is a funny way of doing the washing!

1. *de*. 2. at the time of = *lors de*. 3. *attendre* is followed by *que* alone, instead of *jusqu'à ce que*. 4. omit. 5. *encore* or *de plus*. 6. *faire*. 7. it. 8. *à*. 9. *dans*. 10. the. 11. insert *at*. 12. how. 13. *servent-ils à quelque chose*. 14. why did they put.

EXERCISE XXIV

THE LOIRE VALLEY [1] — BACK IN PARIS (Pages 155-156)

Grammatical study: idioms to express the word "get"; "used to"; uses of the past anterior; predicative *le, la, les; en* meaning "its"; *mouvoir* and *émouvoir, coudre*.

A. 1. When he was told that he had got to leave here, he was greatly moved.

2. Shall you get your house painted this year?

3. We want them to get home early this evening. They may not be tired, but we are.

4. Where did you get what you were sewing when she got here?

5. Who got the prize? Why, don't you know?

6. He used to go and get [2] the newspapers at the store.

7. When she had sewed a button on the boy's coat, she went and got a dress. Is she his mother? She is.

8. He had hardly got out of the house when his friends got here.

9. When you see the new moon, if you say what you want, you will get it.

10. He wanted his mother to sew some buttons on his coat.

11. She is sewing; she has got to do it in order to earn her living. Is she poor? She is.

12. Do not be afraid to ask for what you wish; you will not get it, otherwise.

13. As soon as he had told us how much money he got per week, we said no [3] more. We thought he was rich, but he isn't.

14. What you have done moves him in [4] a strange manner.

15. I am glad you went and got him something to eat.

16. Was he tired? Yes, he was, but as soon as he had got up, he went away.

17. What a pretty hat! Where did you get it?

18. How did you get rid of the flies at your house?

19. He used to know how to get along, whatever he had to do.

20. He used to get money every week; as soon as he had got it, he would spend it.

21. She said what he was doing moved her; he had got those presents without her knowing it. She is his sister, isn't she? She is.

22. They have got along without help so far, but they are getting older.

23. They get their hair cut every [5] three weeks.

24. Those children got their feet wet. Are they good children? They are.

25. When shall you sew the ribbon on that dress? You've got to go and get me some thread so that I may sew it.

B. Well, here we are back at Paris, after traveling several days in the Loire valley. I am glad you took me there. —

Don't you think [6] it's one of the most beautiful parts of France? — Certainly, its castles are charming; its fields and forests are, too. I am glad you showed them to me. — The castles are [7] its principal charm; there are more of them than there are of other things that are worth seeing. All the castles are full of interest. Their architecture is, for the most [8] part, good. — That is true; but what interests me most is [9] the stories of historical events that have taken place in these castles. Although I have got used to studying architecture now, still, when I see a new castle, I ask for its legends and the stories of what has been done there. Each one of these castles that we have just been visiting has its own history of kings and counts, lords and vassals, political prisoners and those who guarded them. I shall remember some of these stories as long as I live. That is why I think the valley of the Loire is [10] so interesting.

Before getting ready to start for the south, I must get some things at some store. — What do you need? — I need a hat, some shoes, and an umbrella. I want also some gloves; for although I do not want to wear any now, I shall need them when I am at home next winter. They are sold [11] so cheap here that it is worth while to buy two or three pairs. Then I shall buy a trunk, for I haven't any. Mine got broken before I got here last year. — You will not take any trunk when we go to the south, will you [12]? — Oh no; as soon as I have packed my trunk, I shall have it registered at the station and send it to Le Havre, whence I shall start for America when I have finished my travels in Europe.

C. I got a letter this morning from a friend of mine [13] in America. He wants me, when I write him again, to describe to him the house in which we live here in Paris, and tell him all the things which seem strange to us. — Goodness! he wants you to write a whole book, doesn't he? We have got accustomed to many of the things that seemed strange at first, for we have been here more than eight months now. But if we think of our first days in Paris, we shall remember our impressions when we had just come into this house for the first time, the day after we got to the city.[14] — I shall tell him first, of course, that we live in a boarding house; that the lady at whose house we live has two apartments, on the third and fourth floors. I shall tell him something about this lady, who shows so much kindness to us and the other boarders. — Does your friend know that there are other boarders? Shall you tell him who these people are [15] who live with us? — I think so.[16] Since there live here two artists, a teacher, one musician, two students, and a young man who came to Paris only to have a good time, I think we have a rather interesting group of people. Here are some of the things in which my friend will be interested, in [17] my opinion; I have made a list of them. First, of course, there is the fireplace in our room; then, the balcony where we have taken our places on warm evenings during the spring; the clothes press, which takes the place of a closet. My friend is used to having running water in his room. I shall tell him that there is nothing of the kind here, but that the maid brings us our [18] warm water every morning. That is not so convenient when we wash and shave. — Shall you tell him anything about the woman [19] downstairs who began to beat her carpets on the balcony one morning at quarter of seven, before it was light? — No, I shall not say anything about her. But she has not done it since. I went down and talked to her frankly. How happy I was that day at being able to scold in French. How angry Madame was at that woman on [4] the second floor [10], who received company before seven o'clock in the morning, and who made so much noise in closing the door afterwards. I never told her who it was, that it was I who had [20] gone down. — You will not tell [21] your friend, either, about the two men who, after spending an evening at some ball, no doubt, were returning home intoxicated; having lost their way, they began to sing and shout in the street under our window, at three o'clock in the morning. I remember how you got up and threw coal at them. You must have hit them, for they went away quickly and never came back. — Yes, and how shocked Madame was when I told her what I had done! She told me those men had a [22] right to do what they wished, and that I had run the risk of being arrested! No, these incidents have nothing to do with life in Paris; but it's little things like these that make life happy.

1. valley of the Loire. 2. inf.; omit *and*. 3. nothing. 4. *de*. 5. all the. 6. *trouver*. 7. *faire*. 8. larger. 9. they are. 10. omit. 11. refl. 12. change sentence to read: *I think that you aren't going to* . . . 13. one of my friends. 14. the next day (*lendemain*) of our arrival. 15. put verb after *qui*. 16. *je crois que oui*. 17. *à*. 18. some. 19. of. 20. what person? 21. *you will say* (or *write*) *nothing*. 22. the.

EXERCISE XXV

FAIRS — THINGS TO SEE IN PARIS (Page 157)

Grammatical study: idioms to express the word "take"; conditional sentences contrary to fact; *quand*, etc., with the conditional in the sense of a past future; *aller, envoyer, acquérir, courir, cueillir, faillir, fuir, haïr, prendre, conduire.*

A. 1. If she had been willing to go with him, he would have taken her to the ball.

2. When he goes to Paris, he will take your new trunk.

3. He said that when he went to Paris, he would borrow it from you.[1]

4. If it didn't take so much money, we should like to take you there with us.

5. He told us that when we sent him those books, he should take only two.

6. If they were picking flowers in the garden, they would see us and run to meet us.[2]

7. Tell him that as soon as he sends us the papers that we need, we shall read them at once.

8. He said he would send them to you as soon as he could.

9. If he studied more often, he would acquire a greater knowledge of the French language.

10. The old lady who has fallen and broken her arm wants you to take her to the doctor's.

11. They do not hate you; if they hated you, they would not have come to take you to the theater.

12. The generals told the soldiers that as soon as they

were told that the enemy was fleeing, they might be sure that the French had conquered.

13. Run quickly, when she calls for [3] help, for I am afraid she has hurt herself.

14. They are sending you these books so that you may have time to [4] read them before you go to Paris.

15. He almost cut off his hand; he said that when he went home, he would tell the doctor what he had done.

16. If that man ran more often and exercised more, he would be better.

17. When he goes to the city, he will buy you something pretty, whatever you say.

18. Didn't you expect that he would buy you something better than that when he went to the city?

19. Whatever they send you, take it without complaining. Take it home with you when you go.

20. I was hoping they would take you with them when they went to Paris; I wanted them to take me too.

B. We have just returned to the house after taking a walk on the outer boulevards. When we started, a little while [5] after lunch, at half past one, we intended to go as far as the boulevards, then to take a street car, so as to get back to the house early; for we have a great many things to do, since we are going to leave Paris next week, to go to Marseilles. But we might have known that when we got to the boulevards, we should find something new, and that we should stay there the whole afternoon. That is what we do each time that we take a walk; and it is what we did to-day. This time it was the gingerbread fair [6] that interested us. It takes place out by [7] the Place de la Nation. Although we had already seen two or three fairs, since the Parisians have several in the spring, still we found enough things there to keep us until six o'clock.

The boulevard of which I speak has a broad sidewalk through the middle of it,[5] which furnishes plenty of room to set up the booths where gingerbread [8] and other things are sold. In the square we found amusements of all sorts, — shooting galleries, merry-go-rounds, trained animals and so on.

We saw a fair when we were in Brittany; this was much more picturesque than those we have seen in Paris. For there one sees all the peasants, men and women, wearing [9] the costumes of the country. Then, such a thing as [10] a fair always has more interest, it seems to me, when it takes place in the country. But those who like to study the life of the people can find no better chance to do it than at the fairs, either in the country or in the city.

C. If we could stay in Paris six months more, I think we should not see all that this city has of interest. Each time that we go out we see something new. Now it is a sign, now a new kind of cart, and so on. Those who think they have done their duty as soon as they have seen the principal public buildings, the monuments, the museums, and the other things of which the guide speaks, are mistaken. They have only begun to see a city; they know only the smaller part of it. I confess to you that when I was making my plans for the trip, I expected to spend in a city only as many days as Baedeker says it is worth. For you must know that this excellent book, which is used by all who travel in Europe, gives us a list of the important things offered by each city that one is to visit, and then we are told that it will take two days, or perhaps [11] two and one-half days, or even a week, to see all there is. My friend and I were saying to each other yesterday that we pitied *any one* who travels [12] that way. Not but what one can see many things in very little time. Most people who travel have only a few weeks to see many places, and have to make the most of the time they have. Understand what I mean. I say nothing of these intelligent travelers who, for [5] lack of time, can make only short visits at [13] a place, but who travel always with [5] their eyes open. I am complaining about those who have nothing important to do, who might stay whole months in an interesting city, studying [14] its life, if they wanted to, but who run from city to [15] city, with [5] their finger in the Baedeker, without paying attention to the life of the people, their customs, their houses, and so on. What is the use of traveling [16]? I think you must have met some of these people, you who know Japan and China, Italy, Switzerland, Germany, Holland, Spain, and so many other foreign countries, without saying anything of the Rocky Mountains, and all the other parts of the United States which are being visited more and more now.

Well, I assure you that my friend and I, who say [17] so many things about those who don't know how to travel, are doing our best to see Paris in the right way.[18] (All that I have said above was to be only the introduction to a list of some of the new things we have just discovered these last few [5] days; but there [19] ! I shall have to put off my description of them to another chapter.)

1. ind. obj. 2. *à notre rencontre*. 3. *à*. 4. *le temps de*. 5. omit. 6. fair of (*à*) the gingerbreads. 7. *du côté de*. 8. plural. 9. who wear. 10. a thing such as. 11. *bien*. 12. insert *de*. 13. *dans*. 14. *à* with inf. 15. *en*. 16. *à quoi bon voyager*. 17. what person? 18. *in the right way = bien*, before inf. 19. *voilà*.

EXERCISE XXVI

ON THE BANKS OF THE SEINE

Grammatical study: idioms to express the words "put" and "marry"; idioms to express "hot," "cold," etc.; *pour* with the infinitive; *en* with the present participle; comparatives; verbs conjugated with *être*; *mourir, ouvrir, partir, tenir, venir, vêtir*.

A. 1. You ought to put on your coat. It is colder than you think, and since you are starting for a cold city, you will be cold if you are not careful.

2. The young man and the young lady who came to see us last summer were married last week.

3. That man is married at last. Which girl did he marry? The one he met at the hotel last summer.

4. They had started before I came, so that I didn't see the girl of whom you are speaking; is she as pretty as the one who married your friend?

5. They came into the house soon after she had gone out. They stayed only a few minutes.

6. When did she die? I am sorry she has died, for the more one saw her, the better he liked her.

7. Pastor Wagner married them in his church in Paris.

8. Have you opened as many boxes of apples as he? By working hard you can open more than he.

9. While coming here, she fell and broke her arm.

10. Open that box now, in order to give some of those apples to the lady who came in a few minutes ago.

11. While covering the plants in her garden, she got her feet wet; she caught cold and died the next day.

12. Those men who arrived yesterday, to buy a house for their friend who is to get married, are very pleasant. I like [1] them more and more.

13. While eating the apples which had been bought for him, he was opening the letters which had come during the morning.

14. The box that I opened contains more bad apples than good ones, — a thing [2] which has happened several times lately.

15. We were expecting to see her before she started; but she started without saying anything to us about it.

16. In order to finish this lesson on time, she came into the house, although she wanted very much [3] to stay in the garden.

17. We came quickly, for we were afraid he would die.

18. They used to come and see us more and more often; but they do not come any longer; they have not come this month.

19. As soon as he had married her, he took her to Europe, where they stayed two months.

20. Is he married or single? Single; he was expecting to be married last month, but the girl he was to marry fell sick and died.

B. Ever [4] since we have been [5] here, we have told each other many times that we intended before we left the city to follow the Seine, beginning at the "New Bridge" (which, by the way, was built in the sixteenth century and is the oldest bridge in Paris) and going as far as possible down the river. There are only a few things to see up the river; the Bois de Vincennes, near the river, the Marne, where it empties into the Seine, outside the city, and inside the city, the wine market, are perhaps the most important. But going down the river, to St. Cloud, there are more interesting places than one could describe even if he wrote a whole book. At last, to-day, we have done what we had intended to do, for such a long time. We started early, so as to have time enough to reach St. Cloud, a pretty little town on the other side of the Bois de Boulogne. First, beginning at the New Bridge, we noticed the wharves which extend along the river on both sides. These have always interested us. Several vessels were unloading there this morning, and we might have stayed there all day, watching [6] them, if we had not known that we should not reach our destination unless [7] we continued on our way. It seems strange to me that there should be wharves here at the very [8] center of the city, right [9] opposite the Louvre.

Another place which we have seen many times, but which, nevertheless, makes us stop each time we pass it, is the public washing place. For you must know that there are in the river little buildings, in [10] the form of pontoons, where many women go to do their washing. Since those whom one sees there are for the most part women of the lower class, who speak French very poorly, it is hard to understand what they say, but one who is in Paris in order to observe the life of the working classes ought to come here from time to time. It is one of the best places in the city for doing this.

C. In the country towns the women do their [11] washing on the banks of the rivers, without using any wash house. Thus, it is much easier to watch them there, since one can approach them without their paying [12] attention. I have sometimes seen a hundred all working [13] together, and talking [13] and laughing [13] as they did the washing.

But "let's come back to our mutton,[14]" as the French say. I cannot mention all the fine buildings which are near one or the other bank of the river. The Louvre, the Hôtel des Invalides, where live many old soldiers, the House of Deputies, are among the most important buildings. Under the dome of the Invalides is the tomb of Napoleon. You remember the inscription, the sentence from his will: "Je désire que mes cendres reposent sur les bords de la Seine au milieu de ce peuple français que j'ai tant aimé." The Eiffel Tower, too, is near the river. There are fine streets along both banks, so that there is no better place to take a walk than here. The numerous bridges, which are crossed [15] by thousands of people and by omnibuses, automobiles, and carriages of all sorts, and the boats which make trips on the river, make the scene very gay.

One of the most striking things which can be seen along this river, is the fishermen, — the famous fishermen of the Seine, who are written about [15] in literature, and who are known to all who have ever visited Paris. What amuses

us is that they hardly ever [16] catch any fish; several times
I have seen them catch little ones, three or four inches
long, but what's the use of catching those? They don't
catch any big fish, simply because there aren't any; how
can one expect a fish to become big enough to be worth
catching, since there are hundreds of men and boys
waiting [13] for it [11], line in [17] hand. There's hardly a fish
but what is [18] caught as soon as his mouth is [19] large
enough to take the hook.

But what of it! A true fisherman told me once he didn't
want to catch any fish; whenever he caught any, he had
to take the fish off [20] the hook, which didn't leave enough
time for fishing. That's [21] what these Parisians must
think. So they stay there, day after day,[22] line in hand and
pipe in mouth, and have a good time, without thinking of
all who stop to watch them, without paying attention to
all that is said [15] to them by the bystanders.

1. use *plaire*. 2. *ce*. 3. *tenir à*. 4. omit. 5. what
tense? 6. *à* with inf. 7. *à moins de* with inf. 8. *même*,
after noun. 9. *tout*. 10. *sous*. 11. the. 12. *faire*.
13. rel. clause. 14. plural. 15. active. 16. almost never.
17. *à*. 18. *qui ne soit*. 19. he has the mouth. 20. take off =
enlever à. 21. *voilà*. 22. *de jour en jour*.

EXERCISE XXVII

WHAT THEY EAT AT PARIS

Grammatical study: negatives; verbs governing dependent
 infinitives, and the prepositions that they require; verbs
 governing complements in ways different from English, such
 as *obéir à, s'approcher de, regarder, payer*; prepositions after

verbs, such as *savoir gré de, penser à; conduire, connaître, coudre, craindre, croire.*

A. 1. He hardly ever drinks any coffee; he stopped drinking it years ago.

2. Nobody can translate French better than he; he wants to teach French.

3. Neither his father nor his mother expects to come.

4. Are they going to start without waiting for us?

5. They have started already; they looked for you, but could not find you.

6. Haven't they anything to do? They have much to do, but they prefer to let others do it.

7. It is a question of knowing how to do what his teacher has taught him.

8. The rain never prevented them from starting; I am afraid they are sick.

9. Pity [1] those who have neither friends nor money.

10. We are thinking of starting for New York to-morrow. I hope you will join us there.

11. There is no longer anybody here; that is, there is nobody whom we know.

12. Take care not to hurt that boy.

13. They had approached her and were laughing at what she had just said.

14. For whom are you waiting? I am waiting for some one to take me to the station.

15. Do not forget to write when you get there; we shall thank you for your letters.

16. That boy ought to obey the lady with whom he is living, but he disobeys her every day.

17. How much did you pay for those apples? I paid four francs and a half for them.

18. I was afraid you had paid too much for them.

19. We congratulate you on your good fortune.

20. Send for me when you need me. I shall never cease being grateful to you for all you have done for me.

21. She trusted him, and he has borrowed a lot of money from her.

22. No one uses, better than he, the talents God has given him.

23. He has decided to wait until they come.

24. He is beginning to eat his lunch without waiting for those who are to come.

25. Do they enjoy their new boat? Yes, they like [2] it very much.

B.* 1. It is of no use for you to tell us you are getting ready to do what you promised to do long ago; we doubt it.

2. Take care not to laugh at them; they would never pardon the one who laughed at them.

3. Are you afraid of him? He won't hurt you at all, but I suppose it is of no use for me to tell you so.

4. In order to get home, they were obliged to borrow money from the only person they knew in this city.

---

* In order to provide more abundant practice in the use of the idioms now being studied, B in Exercises XXVII to XXX, inclusive, consists of separate sentences, such as are contained in A. The sentences in B are more difficult than those in A, but in general the gradation in difficulty between A, B and C, is not so marked here as in the preceding lessons.

FRENCH COMPOSITION

5. What shall you buy of that man? Nothing; I do not need anything.

6. They never play the piano after ten o'clock in the evening; the landlord does not allow it.

7. About whom are you complaining now? Somebody has taken my money from me, and I am complaining of him.

8. How shall you recognize the man who borrowed money from you, when you see him? Oh, I shall have no difficulty.

9. Because they have got along very well so far without what you offered them, they think they will always be able to do without it.

10. Do you want to play tennis? I should rather hear you play the piano. I like to listen to good music.

11. What is the matter? She has caught cold. Her mother was afraid she would, and told her to put on her coat, but she would not obey her.

12. What has become of those whom you introduced to me yesterday? They couldn't wait until you came.

13. When he comes, I hope you will take care not to laugh at him; he doesn't expect to be made fun of.

14. It is of no use for you to complain. They are as anxious as you to do what they can.

15. I never saw anything more beautiful than the sunset I enjoyed last night.

16. Tell him to ask that man for some apples. We want him to buy some.

17. He hasn't any, so it is of no use for you to ask him for some.

104   FRENCH COMPOSITION

18. He wants you to sew a button on his coat. Take pity on him, I beg of you.

19. What would become of her if she should neglect to do what you ordered her to do?

20. Do you expect to be here when they come? No, I am afraid I shall have gone away before they arrive.

C. Since we came to Paris we have got [3] the habit of taking a little lunch toward the end of the afternoon. Not but what we have enough to eat at mealtimes! No, it's not that; we have plenty. Of course, they serve us only rolls and chocolate for breakfast; for those who are accustomed to having meat and potatoes, and so on, at the beginning of the day, that is hardly a meal. As for us, we are very well satisfied with it. But at noon, we always have a most delicious meal. For example, to-day they served us first some hash, then roast beef and potatoes, with string beans and radishes. Sometimes we have cauliflower, which we like [4] very much. Then for dessert, we had, as usual, Dutch cheese and jam; to-day it was raspberry jam that we were given; sometimes it is strawberry jam, or perhaps honey.

But let us "come back to our mutton" (permit me to use the French expression). Although it always seems to us, after taking such a meal, that we shall not need anything more before dinner time, nevertheless I am starving nearly every afternoon before six o'clock. For you remember that dinner is not served until 7.30. Of course, we need something to eat! The lady at whose house we live is not surprised that we should have [3] our lunch in our rooms; she expects it.

FRENCH COMPOSITION 105

What we eat most often is milk chocolate. We like the Swiss milk chocolates very much, and my friend buys some almost every day. If we are not at the house, but are taking a walk when the time for [5] this lunch arrives, we usually buy some little cakes at some one of the shops which are found everywhere. Sometimes we drink a glass of milk in a restaurant, or if we are in [6] the Bois, or in the Champs-Elyseés, we stop at some "café-concert." Of course, one can get tea or coffee there, too, but *I* don't take either.

What we like best is the chestnuts that we used to get in winter. How delicious they are! We used to buy two or three kilos of them every day, and we'd roast them in front of our fire. Madame used to make fun of us; for, taking our places there, while reading or writing, we would put chestnuts either on the hearth, or perhaps on the shovel, to hold them above the fire. You couldn't imagine anything better for a lunch. Of course, there are none now, in [6] the spring, and we have to hunt for something else when we are hungry. And we have no fire, either.

By the way, a few days ago we saw some goats driven [7] through the streets by two mountaineers. These goats had come down from the mountains, — to see the city, no doubt. Whenever anybody asked those who were taking care of them for some milk, they would stop and milk the goats in the street. That is an idea for your lunch.

1. translate in two ways.   2. use *plaire*.   3. *prendre*.
4. use *trouver*.   5. *de*.   6. *à*.   7. relative clause.

EXERCISE XXVIII

MOTHER MICHEL. THE TWO AMERICANS WHO LOST THEIR WAY

Grammatical study: prepositions governing infinitives (continued); words of nationality; numerals, expressions of measure, uses and omission of the articles; uses of the past anterior; *dire, écrire, faire, lire, mettre, moudre, naître, plaire, prendre, résoudre.*

A. 1. Tell the generals to let us know as soon as they have taken that city.

2. Eighty thousand French soldiers have set out for the battle.

3. "War is hell"; we are told that General Sherman said that.

4. Little John is going to become a doctor when he is old enough.

5. He is only eleven years old now; he was born on the sixth of February.

6. Those men whose names you read in the newspapers are both well-known generals.

7. Do you think the French love art better than the Americans?

8. Have them ask their questions of some one who has studied French.

9. That lady speaks Spanish. I heard her speak it yesterday.

10. Although she reads Italian, I do not think she can speak it.

11. Dutch and Russian are two languages which are studied but little in the United States.

12. How is that said in French?

13. That French city is more than three hundred years older than the oldest city in the United States.

14. Captain A has had two thousand men sent to take that city.

15. How many girls have entered that school? There are 201.

16. They have resolved not to sell their French books.

17. The field is seventy-one feet long by ninety-seven feet wide.

18. Little Mary, whose father is a grocer, does not buy any apples; she asks her father for some.

19. Captain B's son is eleven years older than the boy who is becoming [1] a soldier.

20. Doctors and lawyers earn more money than soldiers, do they not?

21. He will buy 250 pounds of that butter if he likes it.

22. The Italian prince's army has retaken that city, after fighting more than six days.

23. Some Swiss speak French, some speak Italian, but most speak German.

24. Which language do you prefer, French or German?

25. French is spoken everywhere in that part of Switzerland.

B. 1. Have the Frenchman write to him what he has just said about the English language.

2. That city has more than two million inhabitants, of whom a hundred thousand are [2] Italians.

FRENCH COMPOSITION

3. They have subscribed to a French newspaper; as soon as it had come this morning they began to read it.

4. Those men who let us read the papers which they had just received are French soldiers.

5. He wants you to read aloud what his friend has written to him; it is French poetry.

6. The French and the English have fought as [3] enemies many times; but now they are fighting as [3] friends, against the Germans.

7. How many Englishmen are there in this city? There are more than eight hundred.

8. How long have you been studying Italian? I have been studying it a little less than three years.

9. Do you like the Italian language? Yes, but I do not understand its constructions very well.

10. When we were in the country, we used to eat a dozen apples every day, and before going to bed we used to drink a glass of milk.

11. Dr. A's daughter has caught cold, and she will ask her father for some medicine.

12. Do you like French novels? Yes, sir, those that I have read have pleased me very much.

13. When we came in, the miller was grinding the wheat; he had ground forty sacks of it already.

14. When you understand French better, I shall have you read that book aloud.

15. If you were a Frenchman, you would be able to speak French better than you speak it now.

16. That man is a miller. Professor A's son saw him grind his wheat a few days ago.

17. Now he says he wants to become a miller. When he knows how to do it, he will grind wheat also.

18. You ought not to wait until we come back; we shan't be here until twelve o'clock to-night.

19. The American studied his French lesson more than three hours this morning; before he finishes it, he will have to study it another hour.

20. I want you to send me a French book which I can read; I have been studying French only two years and a half.

C. Of all the stories which are told to French children, the one that I like best is that of Mother Michel. You have heard the song in which her trials are related. I have bought a beautiful poster which shows her to us, crying [4] out of [5] the window that she has lost her cat. Her house faces a square which is full of people. All this crowd has stopped and is wondering what can have happened to this beloved cat. According to the song Lustucru is especially interested. He tells her that the cat is not lost; which is indeed true, for he has him under his arm; he is carrying him into his shop, in front of which is seen the sign "Rabbit stew a specialty." [6] Poor cat! the next time you appear before your loving mistress, it will be in [7] a form very different from that of former days. It is to be feared [8] that she will not recognize you when she meets you again. That rascal of a [2] Lustucru thinks only of himself, and has stolen you from the most devoted mistress that has ever mourned a cat.

Two young Americans who were traveling in France had gone out to see what there was of interest in Paris. They had been in Paris only a few hours, so that they didn't know its streets very well. They spoke French pretty well, and as they were rather proud of being able to make themselves understood, they had asked more than a hundred questions of the policemen whom they had met while taking their walk. At last it was time to come back to the hotel. But how could they [9] find it? They had walked such a long time, and had turned so many corners, that they did not know which one of the many streets they saw would lead them there. They had lost their way! But there was a policeman crossing [4] the street. So they approached him. At first they thought of telling him the name of the street they were looking for, which would have been the most natural thing they could have done. But no; although they pronounced French pretty well, that was a rather hard word, and they had not looked up its pronunciation in the dictionary. But then they remembered having seen a sign at the corner of the street. By finding the latter they could reach their hotel without difficulty. Nothing more simple! So they asked the policeman how they could get to "la rue Défense d'afficher."

1. *se faire.* 2. omit. 3. *en;* no art. 4. relative clause.
5. *par.* 6. specialty of rabbit stew. 7. *sous.* 8. *il est à craindre.* 9. omit *could they.*

EXERCISE XXIX

MARSEILLES (Pages 160-165)

Grammatical study: uses of numerals in arithmetic, etc.; days of week, dates, etc.; uses of prepositions with adjectives, such as "good to eat," "good to him"; various uses of prepositions, with shades of meaning; *rire, suivre, vaincre, vivre, recevoir, devoir, asseoir, falloir, mouvoir*.

A. 1. It had been snowing for more than eight hours. The roofs were covered with snow, and the streets were full of it.

2. Who came with that man? His wife came with him. Do you know her?

3. Before the concert we had listened to a man in front of the hall, who was discussing politics.

4. The day before his arrival, we had been obliged to leave early.

5. They had been sitting [1] in the garden in front of the house for more than two hours, when we arrived.

6. You ought not to have told him that; you know he is hated by everybody.

7. He was struck with a club by a man who had approached him without making any noise.

8. That gentleman with the blue eyes and the white hair was greatly moved at what you said.

9. Professor A, my friend's father, has his pupils study French verbs in a new way.

10. On Tuesday he will write to us; we shall receive his letter in ten days.

11. Within a week at the most, I shall have to live with the man at whose manners I have laughed so many times.

12. He thought they had made fun of him. They used to laugh at everything he said.

13. Is he still living? He must be more than eighty years old.

14. Raymond Poincaré, president of the French republic, has had many soldiers enrolled since the beginning of the war.

15. Mr. A, the grocer in front of whose shop we saw such fine apples, has received some more.

16. In spring and in summer the fields will be covered with flowers; then we shall sit there every day when it is pleasant.

17. That hat with the pretty blue flowers is your mother's, is it not?

18. The men with whom you were talking Monday must have gone away early on Thursday.

19. On Fridays he always receives a letter from his mother; she writes with black ink and uses blue paper.

20. So I always recognize the letters when I see them. He is always glad to receive them; he lets me read them sometimes.

B. (Students are to translate these problems and give the answers in French.)

1. *Le Malade Imaginaire,* a play by Molière, is sold here at one franc, 95 centimes a volume. If I buy ten copies, how much do I pay for them?

2. Marie-Antoinette, queen of France and wife of

Louis XVI, was born in 1755 and died in 1793. How old was she when she died?

3. Chestnuts are sold in this shop at five cents a pound. I take nineteen pounds. How much do they cost?

4. The grocer sends for some fruit [2] in the country; he receives 21 dozen apples, 14½ dozen pears, 200 peaches, 80 pounds of cherries. He pays 20 cents a dozen for the apples, 30 cents a dozen for the pears, two cents apiece for the peaches, and three cents a pound for the cherries. How much money does he owe the one who sells him this fruit? [2]

To complete this exercise, pupils are to do the multiplication table in French, from one to twelve, thus:

> One times one is one;
> Two times one is two, etc.

Pupils or teacher can easily provide numerous other problems in arithmetic, which will furnish excellent material for practice in numerals, — one of the hardest subjects to be found in the study of French.

C. Marseilles, for more than one reason, is well worth a visit. It is the principal seaport of France; so there are vessels there from nearly all the countries in [3] the world, and of course it is very interesting to see their sailors and to hear them talk. Then, this is the largest city in the south of France, and as it resembles Paris, those who know the latter find Marseilles full of interest. Most of those who come here have never seen the Mediterranean, and naturally are glad to see even this little bit of it; we have heard [4] so much about it, and have read the history of so many great events which have taken place on this sea or on its shores. Its water is very blue, and I am told that it is salter than that of the ocean itself. That may well be, but I must say that if there is this difference, we really didn't perceive it while swimming in the sea! For we found an excellent beach, not far from the center of the city, where there is a public bath house.

We took [5] a little excursion to the Château d'If, situated on [6] a little island in the Mediterranean, [7] a few kilometers from Marseilles. It is here that Edmond Dantès, hero of Dumas' novel, *Le Comte de Monte Cristo*, was kept a prisoner. How can one fail to believe [8] what the novelist tells us, when [9] we are shown the very cell in which Dantès was kept, and the tunnel dug by him in the rock and plaster so that he could converse with his neighbor, Abbé Faria! They no longer let you enter the cell, but you can see it very well.

On the way back to Marseilles, we saw the beautiful church of Notre Dame de la Garde, which rises high above the city, on a great rock. On the steeple there is a beautiful statue of the Virgin, which is said to [10] protect the city. After reaching the city, we went up to this church, using the elevator. The view from here over [11] the sea is most beautiful.

After coming down into the city again, we took a street car and went by the Prado (a wide avenue resembling the Champs-Elysées at Paris) to the Chemin de la Corniche, a boulevard about seven kilometers long, extending along the sea. On the one side is the sea; below, the road; on the other are beautiful houses where the rich people of Marseilles live.

1. what part of the verb? 2. plural. 3. *de*. 4. insert *tell* (*say*). 5. *faire*. 6. *dans*. 7. at. 8. fail to believe = *ne pas croire*. 9. since. 10. *doit*. 11. *sur*.

EXERCISE XXX

TARASCON (Pages 163-164)

Grammatical study: uses of prepositions (continued); idioms to express personal appearance, such as "he has black eyes"; the word "since"; *depuis* and *il y a* with *ne*; *en* with the present participle; *pleuvoir, pouvoir, savoir, valoir, voir, vouloir*.

A. 1. Whatever you may say, we shall wait for her to come, since she wishes it.

2. Since the first of January, she has had only one dress made.

3. You must be hungry; you have not eaten anything for more than eleven hours.

4. He might have come if he had wished; he knew his father wished it.

5. Since she went away, we have received only two letters from her.

6. His hands are very small, but he can play the piano very well.

7. His brother's hair is red, but his is black.

8. His hands are cold; let him warm them before this fire.

9. Before the concert he told his friend that he could not go out that evening.

10. The sidewalks were all covered with ice, and he was afraid of falling.

11. He broke his arm a little before the first of December, by falling on the ice.

12. Since your father hurt his leg, he has not been able to walk without some one's going with him.

13. Before you go away please have that photograph finished.

14. If you do not know how to do it yourself, have it done by some one else.

15. Since she is anxious for us to write her a letter, let us write it to-night.

16. They should have got here a week ago; what has happened?

17. A week from to-day will be the twenty-fifth of January. He will be thirty-six years old on that day.

18. Your sister's eyes are blue, are they not? I haven't seen her for years.

19. I was wondering whether I should recognize her.

20. Yes, she has blue eyes, a high forehead, a small nose and mouth.

21. She must be very pretty; I remember her when she was only six years old.

22. She used to be a pretty child. How old is she?

23. She was born on May 11, 1898.

24. If you are able to come and see us, I shall be glad to introduce you to her.

25. When you can, I hope you will come and see us; we shall be glad to see you.

B. 1. A fortnight ago he was beginning Chapter six in this book, which he borrowed of you; to-day he has finished Chapter fourteen.

FRENCH COMPOSITION 117

2. What day of the month is it to-day? I can never remember the date, even after I have been told.

3. Your cousin says he will come unless it rains; he will start a little before three o'clock in the afternoon.

4. This room is sixteen feet long by thirteen wide; it is four feet wider than yours.

5. At what time do you want the children to go to bed? Exactly at eight o'clock.

6. It has been raining for more than an hour and a half; for half an hour the rain has been freezing as it fell.

7. They got up at nine o'clock this morning; they were visiting friends last evening and they didn't get home until [1] quarter past twelve.

8. We shall have lunch at 12.30; after walking all the morning we shall be hungry, I am sure.[2]

9. When they went away they said they would come and see us when they could; but I have not heard from them for more than a year.

10. He usually has his hair cut every three weeks; but he has a cold now and he has not had it cut for four weeks.

11. How old is that little girl with the blue eyes? Who is she? She is my sister.

12. She is twelve years old; she is four years younger than I am.

13. After putting her little son to bed, that lady always tells him a story before he goes to sleep.

14. Before coming in, we met your mother in front of the house, and talked with her several minutes.

15. If it should rain, should you go to the country? No, we should have the excursion put off until the fourth of July.

16. She must have been glad to see you; she had not seen you for three months.

17. When you know whether you can stay with us or not, let me know.

18. I know now; I cannot stay any longer, but I must go away before six o'clock.

19. Since they started at seven o'clock this morning, they will be here before long, unless something has happened to them.

20. They ought not to have been so long on the way; they should have been here an hour ago. I am afraid something has happened.

C. Where shall we go to-day? Shall we take a trip out of the city? — Is there anything worth seeing near here? — Oh, yes, there are several cities well worth visiting, which can be reached by traveling only an hour or two. For example, there are Arles, Orange, and Nîmes; all of these cities contain Roman antiquities. Those who are interested in such things should not fail to visit them. — Well, I am a little bit interested in them, but unless you have something else to propose to me I think I can get along very well without this trip. — Oh, but what I have mentioned is only a part of what I intend to show you. But let us take the train; there is one that goes at 9.45.

We get out here. — What is the name of this town? — This is Tarascon. — What, the town where my friend,

Tartarin de Tarascon, used to live? — Certainly. All cities which have been made famous by heroes are worth visiting, and since Tartarin is the hero of one of the best stories in modern French literature, this town receives each year many travelers. — It is a small town. There can't [3] be much to see here, except the places frequented by Daudet's hero. — No, no one would ever have heard of this place without Daudet's writing this story. Thanks to him, the little town, with its ancient castle and its peaceful streets, has acquired more fame than it could ever have acquired without him. — Can one see the house where Tartarin lived? — I think so.[4] When I was here a few years ago, it was closed, but we can, at least, see the outside of it. Of course, we cannot be sure that it is his house. I have been told that it is not his house at all, but that the coachmen who were anxious to take as many people as possible to all the places worth seeing, bought this house a few years ago; since that time they have been calling it the *Villa Tartarin;* so everybody wants to see it, and behold,[5] the coachmen are satisfied. — Don't they roll their *r*'s here more than the Parisians do? — Yes, and they make more gestures in speaking, too. This part of France was formerly called Provence; its inhabitants were called "Provençaux." Their own language is "Provençal," a language which is spoken but little now. — I think this town is very interesting. I am glad you brought me here. Since we leave France to-morrow, and start for Italy, I am glad to see something entirely new. We might have stayed at Marseilles all day. We should have had a good time, no doubt, if we had done [6] that;

but as for me, I am sure that I have enjoyed this little excursion much more than I should have enjoyed the buildings and parks that we might have seen in the city.

1. use *ne* . . . *qu'à*. 2. of it. 3. *ne doit pas*. 4. *je crois que oui*. 5. *voilà que*. 6. use pres. part. with *en*.

VOCABULARY

A

a un, une
abbey abbaie *f.*
abdication abdication *f.*
able, to be pouvoir
about de, sur (see grammar); à peu près, presque; (time) vers
above au-dessus de
abridged abrégé
absolutely absolument
accident accident *m.*
accomplish accomplir
according to selon
account compte *m.*; **to take into account** se rendre compte de
accustomed, to get s'accoutumer
acquaintance connaissance *f.*
acquire acquérir
across à travers; **across (the street)** en face, de l'autre côté de la rue
act acte *m.*
actor acteur *m.*
address adresse *f.*
address (*vb.*) s'adresser à
admission admission *f.*
admit admettre
advanced avancé
advantage, to take advantage of profiter de
advertising post colonne (*f.*) d'affichage
afar loin
afford s'offrir
afraid, to be craindre, avoir peur
after (*prep.*) après
after (*conj.*) après que
afternoon après-midi *m.* or *f.*
afterwards plus tard, après
again encore (une fois), de nouveau
against contre
ago il y a (before word modified)
agreeable agréable
agreement accord *m.*
ahead: to be ahead of l'emporter sur
ahead (time) en avance, d'avance
aid aide *f.*, secours *m.*
air air *m.*
alive, to be vivre
all tout
allow permettre
almost presque, à peu près
almost, to have almost + **past part.** faillir + inf.
alone seul
along le long de
aloud à haute voix
Alps Alpes *f. plu.*
already déjà
also aussi
altar autel *m.*
although bien que, quoique
altogether tout à fait
always toujours

121

America Amérique *f.*
American Américain
amount montant *m.*
amuse amuser
amusement amusement *m.*
amusing amusant
ancient ancien
and et
anemone anémone *f.*
angry fâché
animal animal *m.*
announce annoncer
announcement annonce *f.*
another un(e) autre, encore un(e)
answer réponse *f.*
answer (*vb.*) répondre
antiquity antiquité *f.*
anxious, to be tenir à (à ce que)
any (*adj. emphatic*) quelconque (*after noun*)
anybody (*emphatic*) qui que ce soit
anything quelque chose; **not anything** ne . . . rien
anywhere (*emphatic*) où que ce soit
apartment appartement *m.*
apiece la pièce
appear apparaître
apple pomme *f.*
approach s'approcher de
approve approuver
April avril *m.*
architecture architecture *f.*
area superficie *f.*
arise se lever
arm bras *m.*
army armée *f.*
around (*adv.*) autour
around (*prep.*) autour de
arrangement arrangement *m.*
arrest arrêter, pincer
arrival arrivée *f.*
arrive arriver

arrondissement arrondissement *m.*
art art *m.*
artist artiste *m.*
as comme, que; **as . . . as** aussi . . . que; **as many** autant; **as for** quant à; **as long as** tant que; **as soon as** aussitôt que; **as well** également
ashes cendres *f. plu.*
ask demander, prier
asparagus asperge *f.*
assemble s'assembler
at à; **at — 's** chez
attend assister à
attention attention *f.;* **to pay attention** faire attention
attract tirer
Austria Autriche *f.*
author auteur *m.*
autobus autobus *m.*
automobile automobile *f.*
autumn automne *m.* or *f.*
avenue avenue *f.*
avoid éviter
awful affreux

B

back de retour
bad mauvais; **it is too bad** c'est dommage
baggage bagage *m.*
balcony balcon *m.*
ball bal *m.*
banana banane *f.*
bank rive *f.*, bord *m.*
banquet banquet *m.*
bargain marché *m.;* **to make a bargain** conclure un marché
bargain (*vb.*) marchander
basis fond *m.*
basket panier *m.*

Bastille Bastille *f.*
bath house bain *m.*
battoir battoir *m.*
bay baie *f.*
be être; there to be y avoir (there is il y a, etc.)
beach grève *f.*
beam poutre *f.*
bear porter
beat battre
beautiful beau
beautifully à merveille
beauty beauté *f.*
because (*conj.*) parce que
because (*prep.*) à cause de
become devenir; what has become of? qu'est devenu?
bed lit *m.*; go to bed se coucher
before (*prep.*) avant, devant; (*with inf.*) avant de
before (*conj.*) avant que
before (*adv.*) auparavant
beg prier; I beg of you je vous en prie
begin commencer, se mettre à
beginning commencement *m.*
behind derrière
behold voilà
Belgian belge
Belgium Belgique *f.*
believe croire
belong appartenir, être à
beloved bien-aimé
bench banc *m.*
beneath au-dessous de
beside à côté de
besiege assiéger
best (*adj.*) le meilleur
best (*adv.*) le mieux
Bethlehem Bethléem
better (*adj.*) meilleur
better (*adv.*) mieux
better, to be valoir mieux, être meilleur; better, to be (health) se porter mieux

between entre
beyond au delà de
big grand
bind relier
binding reliure *f.*
bird oiseau *m.*
birth naissance *f.*
bit: little bit tout petit peu
black noir
blackbird merle *m.*
blind alley impasse *f.*, cul-de-sac *m.*
blossom fleur *f.*
blossom (*vb.*) fleurir
blue bleu
boarder pensionnaire *m.*
boarding house pension *f.*
boards: bound in boards cartonné
boat bateau *m.*
boating, to go se promener en bateau
body corps *m.*
bold audacieux
book livre *m.*
bookbinder relieur *m.*
booth baraque *f.*
born, to be naître
borrow emprunter
both (tous) les deux
boulevard boulevard *m.*
bound (*vb.*) limiter
bound (*adj.*) relié
box boîte *f.*
boy garçon *m.*
branch branche *f.*
brave brave, courageux
brazier brasier *m.*
break (se) casser
breakfast petit déjeuner *m.*
Breton breton
bridge pont *m.*
bring apporter, conduire, mener
bring up monter

briquette briquette f.
Brittany Bretagne f.
broad large
brother frère m.
bud bouton m.
build bâtir
building bâtiment m., édifice m.
burn brûler
bury enterrer
bus = omnibus m.
bush buisson m.
busy occupé
but mais; **but** (= only) ne . . . que
butter beurre m.
button bouton m.
buy acheter
bystander assistant m.

C

cabbage chou m.
cabinet cabinet m.
cage cage f.
cake gâteau m.
call appeler; **to call on** visiter, faire visite à
can pouvoir
Canada Canada m.
canal canal m.; **Panama Canal** canal de Panama
candidate candidat m.
canton canton m.
capital capitale f.
captain capitaine m.
car wagon m.; char m. (Ex. 22); **street car** tram m.
card carte f.
care soin m.; **to take care of** prendre soin de, garder; **to take care not to** se garder de
careful soigneux
carefully soigneusement
carnival carnaval m.
carp carpe f.

carpentry menuiserie f.
carpet tapis m.
carriage voiture f.
carry porter, emporter
cart charrette f.
case cas m.; (for filing, for books, etc.) casier m.
case: in case en cas que, au cas que
castle château m.
cat chat m.
catalogue catalogue m.
catch prendre; **to get caught** être pris; **to catch cold** s'enrhumer
cathedral cathédrale f.
cauliflower chou-fleur m.
cause cause f.
cause (vb.) causer
cease cesser
ceiling plafond m.
celebrate célébrer
cell cellule f.
cellar cave f.
Celt Celte m.
censor censeur m.
cent sou m.
center centre m.
centime centime m.
central central
centralize centraliser
century siècle m.
certain certain
certainly certainement, certes
chair chaise f.
chance (= opportunity) occasion f.
chance (= luck) 'hasard m.
Channel: English Channel Manche f.
chapel chapelle f.
chapter chapitre m.
character caractère m.
charge: in charge of chargé de
charm charme m.

VOCABULARY

charming charmant
cheap bon marché
cheese fromage *m.*
cherry cerise *f.*
chestnut marron *m.*
chestnut tree marronnier *m.*
chief chef *m.*
child enfant *m.*
China Chine *f.*
chocolate chocolat *m.;* milk chocolate chocolat au lait
choice choix *m.*
choir chœur *m.*
choose choisir
Christ Christ *m.*
Christmas Noël *m.*
church église *f.*
Cinderella Cendrillon *f.*
citizen citoyen *m.;* citoyenne *f.*
city ville *f.*
civil civil
civilization civilisation *f.*
class classe *f.*
classic, classical classique
classic (*n.*) classique *m.*
clean (*vb.*) nettoyer
clean (*adj.*) propre
clear clair
clerk commis *m.*
climate climat *m.*
climb monter; faire l'ascension de
cling se cramponner
clock pendule *f.*
cloister cloître *m.*
close fermer
close to (*adv.*) tout près de
closet cabinet *m.*
clothe vêtir
clothes vêtements *m. plu.*
clothes press armoire *f.*
clothing vêtements *m. plu.*
club massue *f.*
coachman cocher *m.*
coal charbon *m.*

coast côte *f.*
coat habit *m.*
coffee café *m.*
cold froid; to be cold (person) avoir froid; to be cold (weather) faire froid; to catch cold s'enrhumer; to have a cold être enrhumé
colleague colleaborateur *m.*
collection collection *f.*
college collège *m.*
colonial colonial
come venir; to come away partir; to come back revenir; to come home revenir à la maison; to come in entrer; to come out sortir; to come out (buds) poindre; to come together se réunir, s'assembler; to come up monter.
come near, to have, + *vb. in -ing* faillir + inf.
comfortable commode
commence commencer
commune commune *f.*
company du monde
comparison comparaison *f.*
compartment compartiment *m.*
complain se plaindre
complete complet
completely complètement, tout à fait
complicated compliqué
concern concerner
concerning sur, à l'égard de, à propos de
concert concert *m.*
conductor receveur *m.*
confess avouer
confused confus
congratulate féliciter
connect relier
connection connection *f.*
conquer vaincre

considerable considérable
consideration, to take into se rendre compte de
constitution constitution *f.*
construction construction *f.*
consul consul *m.*
contain contenir
continue continuer
contrary contraire
control contrôler
convenient commode
conversation conversation *f.*
converse causer
cook cuire
cool (*vb.*) refroidir
copy (painting, etc.), copie *f.*; (book, etc.) exemplaire *m.*
cord corde *f.*
corner coin *m.*, angle *m.*
correspond correspondre
cost coûter
costume costume *m.*
council conseil *m.*
count comte *m.*
countess comtesse *f.*
country pays *m.*
country town ville (*f.*) de province
couple: a couple of deux
courage courage *m.*
course cours *m.*
course, of bien entendu; c'est vrai
court house palais (*m.*) de justice
cousin cousin *m.*, cousine *f.*
cover couvrir
crack fente *f.*
cracker biscuit *m.*
cradle berceau *m.*
crazy fou
crocus crocus *m.*
cross croix *f.*
cross (**through**) traverser
cross road carrefour *m.*
crowd foule *f.*
cry (*n.*) cri *m.*
cry (*vb.*) s'écrier, crier (Ex. 28)
Cuba Cuba
cuckoo coucou *m.*
culture culture *f.*
cup tasse *f.*
curious curieux
curtain rideau *m.*
custom coutume *f.*
customs mœurs *f. plu.*
customs official douanier *m.*
cut couper; **to cut off** couper, découper
cutlet côtelette *f.*

D

damage dégâts *m. plu.*
damp humide; **to be damp** faire humide
dangerous dangereux
dark, to be faire obscur, faire nuit
date date *f.*
day jour *m.*, journée *f.*; **day before** veille (*f.*) de; **day after day** de jour en jour
dead mort
deal: a good deal beaucoup, bien de
dear cher
debt dette *f.*
deceive tromper, décevoir
December décembre *m.*
decide décider
declare déclarer
decorate décorer
decoration décor *m.*
deep profond
defeat vaincre
degree degré *m.*; **degree** (from university) diplôme *m.*; **doctor's degree** doctorat *m.*
delicious délicieux

delivery distribution *f.*
demand demander
democracy démocratie *f.*
deny nier
department département *m.*
deputy député *m.;* **House of Deputies** Chambre (*f.*) des Députés
descend descendre
describe décrire
description description *f.*
desire désirer
dessert dessert *m.*
destination but *m.*, destination *f.*
destroy détruire
detract (from) nuire (à)
devoted dévoué
dictionary dictionnaire *m.*
die mourir
difference différence *f.*
different différent
difficult difficile
difficulty difficulté *f.*
dig creuser
dike digue *f.*
dinner dîner *m.*
direction direction *f.*
directly directement
disagreeable désagréable
discouraged découragé
discover découvrir
discuss discuter
disguise déguiser
dishes vaisselle *f.*
disobey désobéir
divide diviser
do faire; **to do without** se passer de
doctor médecin *m.*
doll poupée *f.*
dollar dollar *m.*
dome dôme *m.*
door porte *f.*
doubt (*vb.*) douter (de)

delightful charmant
doubt (*n.*) doute *m.;* **no doubt** sans doute
down (stream) en aval
downstairs en bas
dozen douzaine *f.*
draught courant (*m.*) d'air
dress robe *f.*
dress s'habiller, vêtir
drink boire
drive chasser; **to drive away** chasser
drunk ivre
dry sec
dummy mannequin *m.*
during pendant
Dutch hollandais
duty devoir *m.*
duty (tax) droit *m.*

E

each chaque
each one chacun; **each other** l'un l'autre
early de bonne heure; **earlier** plus de bonne heure
earn gagner
easily facilement
east est *m.*
easy facile
eat manger; **to eat** (a meal, breakfast, etc.) prendre
economical économe
edition édition *f.*
edge bord *m.*
education éducation *f.*
effect effet *m.*
either l'un ou l'autre; **either... or** soit... soit, ou... ou
either (*after a negative*) non plus
elders aînés *m. plu.*
elect élire
electoral electoral

elevator ascenseur *m.*
else d'autre; some one else quelqu'un d'autre
embrace embrasser
embroider broder
emperor empereur *m.*
emphasize appuyer sur
empire empire *m.*
empty (river) déboucher
enamel émail *m.; plu.,* émaux
encyclopedia encyclopédie *f.*
end fin *f.*
end finir, aboutir (Ex. 22)
ending fin *f.*
enemy ennemi *m.*
English anglais
Englishman Anglais *m.*
enjoy jouir de
enormous énorme
enough assez
enough, to be suffire
enroll enrôler
enter entrer (dans)
entirely tout à fait
entrance entrée *f.*
equally également
erect ériger
escape s'échapper (à)
especially surtout
establishment établissement *m.*
estate état *m.*
Europe Europe *f.*
even même
evening soir *m.*
event événement *m.;* fait *m.*
ever jamais; ever so little tant soit peu
every chaque; tous, toutes les (*noun in plural*); tout, toute (*noun singular, without article*)
everybody tout le monde *m.*
every one tout le monde *m.*
everything tout *m.*
everywhere partout

evident évident
evidently évidemment
exact exact
exactly: eight o'clock exactly huit heures précises
examination examen *m.*
examine examiner
example exemple *m.;* for example par exemple
excellent excellent
except excepté
excursion excursion *f.*
excuse pardonner; excuse me pardon
exercise exercice *m.*
exercise (*vb.*) s'exercer, faire l'exercice
expect s'attendre à (à ce que)
expenses frais *m. plu.*
expensive coûteux, cher
explain expliquer
exposition exposition *f.*, salon *m.*
expression expression *f.*
extend s'étendre
extreme extrême
eyes yeux *m. plu.*

F

face (*n.*) visage *m.*
face (*vb.*) donner sur
fail faillir, manquer
fair foire *f.*
fairy tale conte (*m.*) de fées
fall tomber
fall automne *m.* or *f.*
fame renommée *f.*
family famille *f.*
famous fameux
far loin; as far as jusqu'à
farm ferme *f.*
farmer fermier *m.*
fast (*adv.*) vite

VOCABULARY

father père *m.*
fatherland patrie *f.*
favorite favori
fear craindre
February février
feed nourrir
feel (se) sentir
feeling sentiment *m.*
fellow garçon *m.*
festival fête *f.*
few (*adj.*) quelques, peu (de), rares
few (*pron.*) quelques-uns, -unes, peu
fewer moins (de)
field champ *m.*
fig figue *f.*
fight se battre
fill remplir
finally enfin
find trouver; **to find out** apprendre, savoir
find one's way about s'orienter
fine beau
finger doigt *m.*
finish finir
fire feu *m.*, incendie *m.*
fireman pompier *m.*
fireplace cheminée *f.*
first (*adj.*) premier; **in the first place** (*adv.*) d'abord
fish poisson *m.*
fisherman pêcheur *m.*
fishing pêche *f.*
flag drapeau *m.*
Flanders Flandre *f.*
flee fuir, s'enfuir
Flemish flamand
floor plancher *m.*
flower fleur *f.*
fly mouche *f.*
follow suivre
folly folie *f.*
foot pied *m.*; **on foot** à pied

for (*conj.*) car
for (*prep.*) pour (see grammar)
forbid défendre
forehead front *m.*
foreign étranger
foreigner étranger *m.*
foresight prévoyance *f.*
forest forêt *f.*
forget oublier
form (se) former, (se) faire; **to form in line** se mettre en file
formality formalité *f.*
former, the celui-là
former days autrefois
formerly autrefois
fortnight quinze jours
fortune, good fortune bonheur *m.*
found fonder
fountain fontaine *f.*
franc franc *m.*
France France *f.*
Franco-Prussian franco-allemand
frankly franchement
free (open) libre; (at no expense) gratuit
freeze geler; **to freeze over** geler
French français
Frenchman Français *m.*
frequent fréquenter
Friday vendredi *m.*
friend ami *m.*
frightful affreux
from de; (time) depuis
front: **in front of** devant
fruit fruit *m.*
fruit tree fruitier *m.*
full plein
fun badinage *m.*
fun: **to make fun of** se moquer de
funny drôle
furnish fournir

furniture meubles *m. plu.*; mobilier *m.*
further plus loin
furze ajonc *m.*

G

gallery galerie *f.*
garden jardin *m.*
gate porte *f.*
gay gai
general (*n.*) général *m.*
general (*adj.*) général; **in general** en général
Geneva Genève *f.*
gentleman monsieur; *plu.* messieurs
geography géographie *f.*
German allemand
Germany Allemagne *f.*
gesture geste *m.*
get se procurer, acheter; (an idea) se former; (have got = to have to) falloir; (= to have + past part.) faire + inf.; (= to become) devenir; (= to arrive) arriver; **to get along** se tirer d'affaires; **to get along without** se passer de; **to get down on** se mettre à; **to get in** entrer; **to get out** descendre; **to get rid of** se débarrasser de; **to get to sleep** s'endormir; **to get up** se lever; **to get accustomed to, used to** s'accoutumer à; **to get broken** se casser; **to get married** se marier; **to get ready** se préparer; **to get wet** se mouiller; etc.
gingerbread pain (*m.*) d'épice
girl (jeune) fille *f.*
give donner
give up renoncer à
glad heureux, content

glass verre *m.*
glory gloire *f.*
glove gant *m.*
go aller; **to go away, off** partir, s'en aller; **to go around** faire le tour de; **to go down** descendre; **to go in** entrer; **to go out** sortir; **to go out (fire)** s'éteindre; **to go out (tide)** baisser; **to go through** traverser, parcourir; **to go to bed** se coucher; **to go to sleep** s'endormir; **to go up** monter; **to go up to** s'approcher de; **to go with** accompagner; **to go** (= to become) devenir
goat chèvre *f.*
God Dieu *m.*
gold or *m.*
good bon, sage (of children)
goodness! mon Dieu!
good night bonsoir
Gothic gothique
govern gouverner
government gouvernement *m.*
grape raisin *m.*
grateful reconnaissant
grateful, to be savoir gré
great grand; **great deal, great many** beaucoup
Great Britain Grande Bretagne *f.*
greatly fort, bien
grind moudre
grocer épicier *m.*
ground terre *f.*
group groupe *m.*
grow pousser; (*causative*) faire pousser
guard garder
guess deviner
guide guide *m.*
guillotine guillotine *f.*
Gulf Stream gulf stream *m.*

H

habit habitude *f.*, coutume *f.*
hair cheveux *m. plu.*
half (*adj.*) demi
half (*n.*) moitié *f.*
half-hour demi-heure *f.*
hall salle *f.*
hand main *f.*
hang pendre
happen arriver
happy heureux
hard (*adj.*) difficile
hard (*adv.*) dur, ferme
hardly à peine, ne . . . guère
harm nuire à
hash 'hachis *m.*
hat chapeau *m.*
hate 'haïr
have avoir, **to have to** falloir, devoir
head tête *f.*
hear entendre; **to hear from them** avoir de leurs nouvelles
hearth foyer *m.*
heat chaleur *f.*
heat (*vb.*) chauffer
heather bruyère *f.*
heating chauffage *m.*
Heavens! mon Dieu!
hedge 'haie *f.*
Helena Hélène *f.*
hell enfer *m.*
help aider; **to help one's self** se servir
help (= prevent) empêcher
hence aussi, ainsi
here ici; **here is, here are** voici
hero 'héros *m.*
hidden caché
high 'haut; cher; **high up** bien haut
historic, historical historique
history histoire *f.*

hit frapper
holiday fête *f.*, jour férié *m.*
Holland 'Hollande *f.*
home: **at home** chez moi, lui, elle, etc.
honey miel *m.*
hook hameçon *m.*
hope espérer
horn cor *m.*
horse cheval *m.*
horse back, on à cheval
hotel hôtel *m.*
hour heure *f.*
house maison *f.*
house owner propriétaire *m.*
how comment, comme; **how much, how many** combien
however pourtant
however (*with an adj.*) quelque . . . que; **however that may be** quoiqu'il en soit
hundred cent; (*collective*) centaine *f.*
hungry, **to be** avoir faim
hunt (for) chercher
hurry se dépêcher, se presser
hurry: **in a hurry** pressé
hurt faire mal à, nuire à

I

idea idée *f.*
if si
imagine s'imaginer
impair nuire à
impatiently avec impatience
importance importance *f.*
important important
impression impression *f.*
in dans, en, à (see grammar)
inch pouce *m.*
incident incident *m.*
incoming (tide) montant
indeed bien, en effet
independent indépendant

industrious industrieux
industry industrie *f.*
inhabitant habitant *m.*
injured blessé
ink encre *f.*
inscription inscription *f.*
inside (*adv.*) dedans
inside (*prep.*) dans
inside (*n.*) intérieur *m.*
inspect visiter
inspector inspecteur *m.*; (customs) douanier *m.*
inspire inspirer
install installer
instance: for instance par exemple
instruction instruction *f.*
insurance company compagnie (*f.*) d'assurances
insure assurer
intelligent intelligent
intend avoir l'intention (de)
interest intéresser; **to be interested in** s'intéresser à
interest intérêt *m.*
interesting intéressant
intoxicated ivre
introduce présenter
introduction introduction *f.*
invite inviter
island île *f.*; îlot *m.* (Ex. 22)
Italian italien
Italy Italie *f.*
ivy lierre *m.*

J

jam confiture *f.*
janitor concierge *m.*
janitress concierge *f.*
Japan Japon *m.*
Jesus Jésus *m.*
jewel bijou *m.*
Joan Jeanne *f.*
John Jean *m.*
join se joindre à

Joseph Joseph *m.*
journey voyage *m.*
judge juge *m.*
judge juger
July juillet *m.*
June juin *m.*
just (*adv.*) exactement
just: to have just (+ past part.) venir de (+ inf.)

K

keep garder, tenir, retenir; **to keep from** empêcher de
keep up maintenir
kill tuer
kilo (**kilogram**) kilo (kilogramme) *m.*
kilometer kilomètre *m.*
kind sorte *f.*
kindness bonté *f.*
king roi *m.*
kingdom royaume *m.*
knee genou *m.*
knitting tricotage *m.*
knock over renverser
know savoir, connaître; **to know how** savoir
knowledge connaissance *f.*
known connu

L

lace dentelle *f.*
lack manque *m.*; **for lack of** faute de
lacking, to be manquer
lady dame *f.*
lake lac *m.*
lamb mouton *m.*
lamp lampe *f.*
land! ma foi! mon Dieu! etc.
landlord propriétaire *m.*
language langue *f.*
large grand

lark alouette *f.*
last dernier, passé; at last enfin
late tard
later plus tard
Latin latin
latitude latitude *f.*
latter, the celui-ci
laugh rire
lawyer avocat *m.*
lead conduire, mener
leaf feuille *f.*
learn apprendre
least: at least au moins, du moins
leave laisser, quitter, partir de
lecture conférence *f.*
left gauche
left, to be rester
leg jambe *f.*; (of meat) gigot *m.*
legend légende *f.*
less moins
lesson leçon *f.*
let laisser, permettre
letter lettre *f.*
lettuce laitue *f.*
library bibliothèque *f.*
lie down se coucher
life vie *f.*
light allumer
light, to be faire jour
like aimer; plaire à (see grammar)
like (*adv.*) comme
lilac lilas *m.*
lily of the valley muguet *m.*
line ligne *f.*; in line en file
list liste *f.*
listen to écouter
literature littérature *f.*
little (*adj.*) petit
little (*adv.*) peu; ever so little tant soit peu
live demeurer, vivre; long live vive
live (*adj.*) vivant

lively vif
living vie *f.*
loan prêter
Loire Loire *f.*
long (*adj.*) long
long (*adv.*): long time longtemps; longer plus longtemps; as long as tant que
long (*vb.*) tarder (*impersonal*); we long to il nous tarde de + inf.
longer: no longer ne ... plus
look at regarder
look for chercher
look out not to se garder de
look over feuilleter
look up chercher
lord seigneur *m.*
lose perdre; to lose one's way s'égarer
lot: a lot of beaucoup
Louvre Louvre *m.*
love aimer
loving (*adj.*) aimant
low bas
lower inférieur
loyal loyal
luckily heureusement
lunch, luncheon déjeuner *m.*, goûter *m.*
Luxemburg Luxembourg *m.*
lycée lycée *m.*

M

made: to be made up of consister en
magnificent magnifique
maid bonne *f.*
mail courrier *m.*
mainland terre *f.*
make faire; to make + adj. rendre; to make the most of profiter autant que possible de

VOCABULARY

make marque *f.*
man homme *m.*
manger crèche *f.*
manner manière *f.*
manufacture fabrication *f.*; *plu. collectively* produits fabriqués *m. plu.*
manuscript manuscrit *m.*
many, great many beaucoup, bien (see grammar)
March mars *m.*
market marché *m.*, 'halles *f. plu.*
Marne Marne *f.*
married marié
marry épouser, marier, se marier (see grammar)
marvelous merveilleux
marvelously merveilleusement
Mary Marie *f.*
masked masqué
masquerade (*adj.*) masqué
mass messe *f.*
masterpiece chef-d'œuvre
match allumette *f.*
mathematics mathématique *f.*
matter: what's the matter? qu'avez-vous, qu'y a-t-il
May mai *m.*
may pouvoir, se pouvoir (see grammar); **that may well be** ça se peut bien
mayor maire *m.*
meal repas *m.*
mean vouloir dire, signifier
meaning signification *f.*
means: by means of au moyen de
meat viande *f.*
mechanic mécanique
medicine médecine *f.*
Mediterranean Méditerranée *f.*
meet (by chance) rencontrer; (= to know) connaître
memory mémoire *f.*

mention faire mention de, mentionner
merit mériter
merry-go-round chevaux (*m. plu.*) de bois
messenger, messager *m.*
meter mètre *m.*
Mexico Mexique *m.*
middle milieu *m.*
middle ages moyen âge *m.*
midnight minuit *m.*
might pouvoir (see grammar)
mild doux
milk lait *m.*
milk traire
miller meunier *m.*
million million *m.*
mind esprit *m.*
mind: never mind n'importe
minister ministre *m.*
ministry ministère *m.*
minute minute *f.*
mirror miroir *m.*
miserable misérable
miss manquer
mistake, to make a, to be mistaken se tromper
mistletoe gui *m.*
mistress maîtresse *f.*
model modèle *m.*
modern moderne
moment moment *m.*
Monday lundi *m.*
money argent *m.*
month mois *m.*
monument monument *m.*
moon lune *f.*
Moor Maure *m.*
more plus; **more and more** de plus en plus; **the more . . . the more** plus . . . plus
morning matin *m.*
most le plus; **most (of)** + noun la plupart de; **the most part** la plupart

VOCABULARY

mother mère *f.*
mount mont *m.*
mountain montagne *f.*
mountaineer montagnard *m.*
mourn pleurer
mouth bouche *f.*
move émouvoir
much beaucoup
muffler couvre-col *m.*
municipal municipal
museum musée *m.*
music musique *f.*
musician musicien *m.*
must devoir, falloir (see grammar)
mutton mouton *m.*
my! ma foi!

N

name nom *m.*
nap somme *m.*
Napoleon Napoléon
narrow étroit
national national
natural naturel
naturally naturellement
nature nature *f.*
nave nef *f.*
near près de
nearly presque
necessary nécessaire; **to be necessary** falloir
neck cou *m.*
need (*vb.*) avoir besoin de, falloir
neglect négliger
neighbor voisin *m.*
neighboring environnant
neither ni l'un ni l'autre; neither . . . nor ni . . . ni.
nephew neveu *m.*
never ne . . . jamais
nevertheless néanmoins, pourtant

new nouveau, neuf
New Year's Day le jour de l'an
news nouvelles *f. plu.*
newspaper journal *m.*
next prochain
next day lendemain *m.*; **next morning** le lendemain matin
night nuit *f.*, soir *m.*; **last night** hier soir
night before veille *f.* (de)
nightingale rossignol *m.*
no non
nobody ne . . . personne
noise bruit *m.*
none ne . . . aucun, ne . . . nul
noon midi *m.*
Normandy Normandie *f.*
north nord *m.*
northern septentrional
nose nez *m.*
not ne . . . pas; non (Ex. 29)
not but what non que
nothing ne . . . rien
notice remarquer, observer; **to take notice of** se rendre compte de
novel roman *m.*
novelist romancier *m.*
November novembre *m.*
now maintenant; **now . . . now** tantôt . . . tantôt
number numéro *m.*, chiffre *m.*, nombre *m.*
numerous nombreux

O

oath serment *m.*
obey obéir (à)
oblige obliger
observe observer
ocean océan *m.*
o'clock heure(s) *f.*
of de

off there là-bas
offer offrir
office bureau *m.*
often souvent
old vieux; **to be — years old** avoir — ans, être âgé de — ans
omelet omelette *f.*
omnibus omnibus *m.*
once une fois; **at once** tout de suite; **once in a while** de temps en temps
one (*indef. pron.*) on; (*num.*) un, une; **the one** celui
only seulement; ne . . . que
onto sur
open ouvrir; **open onto** donner sur
open ouvert; **open fire** feu de cheminée
opinion avis *m.*, opinion *f.*
oppose s'opposer à, tenir tête à
opposite en face de
orange orange *f.*
order ordre *m.*
order (*vb.*) ordonner, commander
order: in order to pour, afin de
ordinarily ordinairement
ordinary ordinaire
organization organisation *f.*
other autre
otherwise sinon, autrement
ought devoir
outdoors au-dehors
out of hors de
outer extérieur
outside of hors de
over au-dessus de
over there là-bas
overcast couvert
owe devoir
own propre
own (*vb.*) posséder
owner propriétaire *m.*

P

pack (a trunk) faire (une malle)
pad bourrelet *m.*
page page *f.*
paint peindre
painter peintre *m.*
painting peinture *f.*
pair paire *f.*
palace palais *m.*
Pantheon Panthéon *m.*
paper papier *m.*
paper covered broché
parcel post colis postaux *m. plu.*
pardon pardonner
Parisian parisien
park parc *m.*
part partie *f.*
participle participe *m.*
pass passer; **pass through** parcourir
passage passage *m.*
passage-way passage *m.*
past passé
pastor pasteur *m.*
pastry pâtisserie *f.*
path sentier *m.*
patience patience *f.*
patron patron *m.*, patronne *f.*
pay (for) payer; **pay attention** faire attention
peaceful paisible
peach pêche *f.*
pear poire *f.*
peas petits pois *m. plu.*
peasant paysan *m.;* **peasant woman** paysanne *f.*
peculiar particulier
pen plume *f.*
penetrate pénétrer
penitence pénitence *f.*
pension pension *f.*
people peuple *m.;* gens *m.* or *f. plu.* (see grammar), personnes *f. plu.*, monde *m.;* on

pepper poivre *m.*
per par
perceive s'apercevoir (de)
perfect parfait
performance représentation *f.*
perhaps peut-être
permit permettre
person personne *f.*
photograph photographie *f.*
piano piano *m.*
pick cueillir
pick out choisir
pick up ramasser
picture tableau *m.*
picturesque pittoresque
piece morceau *m.*, pièce *f.*
pile tas *m.*
pilgrimage pèlerinage *m.*
pine tree pin *m.*
pious pieux
pipe pipe *f.*
pity plaindre
pity : it is a pity c'est dommage ; **what a pity** quel dommage
place lieu *m.*, endroit *m.;* **to take place** avoir lieu ; **to take one's place** s'installer ; **to take the place of** remplacer
plague peste *f.*
plan plan *m.*
plant plante *f.*
plaster plâtre *m.*
platform plate-forme *f.*
play (*vb.*) jouer
play pièce *f.;* **plays** (*collectively*) théâtre *m. s.*
pleasant agréable
pleasant, to be (weather) faire beau (temps) ; **to be pleasant (to do something)** faire bon faire quelque chose
please plaire (à) ; = **if you please** s'il vous plaît, veuillez (see grammar); **as they please** comme bon leur semble

pleasure plaisir *m.*
plenty assez, beaucoup, bien
pneumatic pneumatique
poem poème *m.*
poet poète *m.*
poetry poésie *f.*
point point *m.*
police police *f.*
policeman sergent de ville *m.*
political politique
politics politique *f.*
pond mare *f.*
pontoon ponton *m.*
poor pauvre
poorly mal
population population *f.*
port-folio serviette *f.*
position position *f.*
possession possession *f.*
possible possible
postage due surtaxe *f.*
postage stamp timbre-poste *m.;* (*plu.* timbres-poste)
postal postal
posted, to be avoir des renseignements (sur)
poster affiche *f.*
postman facteur *m.*
post office poste *f.*, bureau (*m.*) de postes
posts postes *f. plu.*
potato pomme de terre *f.*
pound livre *f.*
power pouvoir *m.*
Prado Prado *m.*
preach prêcher
preacher prédicateur *m.*
prefect préfet *m.*
prefecture préfecture *f.*
prefer préférer
prepare préparer
present (*adj.*) présent, actuel
present (*vb.*) présenter
present (*n.*) cadeau *m.*
president président *m.*

pretty joli
pretty well (*adv.*) assez bien
prevent empêcher
price prix *m.*
priest prêtre *m.*
prince prince *m.*
principal principal
principal principal *m.*
print imprimer
prison prison *f.*
prisoner prisonnier *m.*
prize prix *m.*
probably probablement, sans doute
procession procession *f.*, monôme *m.*
procure se procurer
product produit *m.*
professor professeur *m.*
profit profiter
program programme *m.*
promise promettre
pronounce prononcer
pronunciation prononciation *f.*
propose proposer
protect protéger
Protestant protestant
proud fier
prove prouver
Provence Provence *f.*
provided (that) pourvu que
province province *f.*
provision provision *f.*
Prussia Prusse *f.*
public public
punish punir
pupil élève *m.*
purse bourse *f.*
pursue poursuivre
push pousser
pull (up) tirer
put mettre; to put off remettre; to put on mettre; to put out éteindre; to put to bed coucher; to put up mettre

Q

quantity quantité *f.*
quarter quart *m.*; quartier *m.*
queen reine *f.*
question question *f.*; to be a question of s'agir de
quickly vite
quiet: to keep quiet, se taire
quite assez, tout

R

rabbit stew civet *m.*
radish radis *m.*
rain pluie *f.*
rain (*vb.*) pleuvoir
raise faire pousser
rarely rarement
rascal vaurien *m.*, diable *m.*
raspberry framboise *f.*
rather plutôt; **rather** (= somewhat) un peu
ravine ravine *f.*
ravishing ravissant
reach arriver à
read lire
ready prêt
real vrai
really vraiment
reason raison *f.*
receive recevoir
recent récent
recently récemment
recite réciter
recognize reconnaître
recommend recommander
rector recteur *m.*
red rouge
reduced réduit
reëstablish rétablir
reference référence
refuse refuser
regard: in regard to sur, à l'égard de

VOCABULARY

register enregistrer, marquer (thermometer)
regular régulier
reign régner
relate raconter
relatively relativement
religion religion *f.*
religious religieux
remain rester
remember se souvenir de, se rappeler
renaissance renaissance *f.*
reply réponse *f.*
reply (*vb.*) répondre (à)
represent représenter
representation représentation *f.*
representative représentant *m.*
republic république *f.*
resemble ressembler
reserve réserver
resolve résoudre
respectful respectueux
rest reste *m.;* les autres *plu.*
restaurant restaurant *m.*
retake reprendre
return revenir
revolution révolution *f.*
ribbon ruban *m.*
rich riche
riches richesse *f.*
ride parcours *m.*
right, to be avoir raison
right droit *m.*
right (*adj.*) droit
right away tout de suite; all right très bien
rise se lever; (tide) monter
risk risque *m.*
river fleuve *m.*, rivière *f.*
road route *f.*
roam errer
roast rôtir
roast beef rosbif *m.*
rock rocher *m.*
rocky rocheux

roll petit pain *m.*
Roman romain
roof toit *m.*
room chambre *f.*, salle *f.;* place *f.*
rose rose *f.*
rule règle *f.*
rule (*vb.*) régner
run courir
running (*adj.*) coulant
Russian russe

S

sack sac *m.*
sailor matelot *m.*
saint saint *m.*, sainte *f.*
salad salade *f.*
salt sel *m.*
salt (*adj.*) salé
sand sable *m.*
satisfied content; to be satisfied se contenter (de)
saucer soucoupe *f.*
Savoy Savoie *f.*
say dire; say! dites-moi, dites donc (*colloquial*)
scarcely à peine, ne . . . guère
scare effrayer
scarf écharpe *f.*
scene scène *f.*
school école *f.*
schoolboy collégien *m.*
science science *f.*
scold gronder
sculpture sculpture *f.*
sea mer *f.*
seaport port (*m.*) de mer
season saison *f.*
seat place *f.*
second deuxième
second-hand d'occasion
secret secret
section section *f.*
see voir

140 VOCABULARY

seem sembler
Seine Seine *f.*
sell vendre
senate sénat *m.*
send envoyer; **to send for** envoyer chercher
sentence phrase *f.*
separate (se) séparer
September septembre *m.*
serious sérieux
servant bonne *f.*, domestique *m.* or *f.*
serve servir; **to serve as** servir de
service service *m.*; culte *m.*
set out partir, se mettre en marche
set to work se mettre à travail
set up établir
settle s'établir
several plusieurs
severe sévère, dur
sew coudre
sewing couture *f.*
shave (se) raser
sheep mouton *m.*
shelf rayon *m.*
shepherd berger *m.*
shine briller
shiver grelotter
shocked choqué
shoe soulier *m.*
shooting gallery galerie (*f.*) de tir
shop boutique *f.*
shore bord *m.* (de la mer)
short court
shout crier, hurler
shovel pelle *f.*
show (*vb.*) montrer
show (*n.*) spectacle *m.*
shut up renfermer
sick malade
side bord *m.*, côté *m.*
sidewalk trottoir *m.*

siege siège *m.*
sign affiche *f.*
sign (*vb.*) signer
signboard plaque indicatrice *f.*
signify signifier
silk soie *f.*
simple simple
simply simplement
since (*prep.*) depuis
since (*conj.*) depuis que; puisque, comme
sing chanter
single seul; (= **unmarried**) garçon
sir monsieur
sister sœur *f.*
sit (down) s'asseoir; **sitting** = p. p. assis; **sit down again** se rasseoir
site emplacement *m.*
situated situé
sketches: **travel sketches** scènes (*f.*) de voyage
skillful habile
sky ciel *m.*
slang argot *m.*
sleep dormir; **to go to sleep, to get to sleep** s'endormir
sleigh-riding, **to go** se promener en traîneau
slip bulletin *m.*
slippery glissant
slung over the shoulders en écharpe (sur l'épaule)
smile sourire
smoke fumer
snow (*vb.*) neiger
snow neige *f.*
so ainsi, aussi; **so that** pour que, afin que; de sorte que, si bien que (see grammar); si; **so . . . as** si . . . que; **and so on** et ainsi de suite
so many, so much tant
sober sobre

VOCABULARY

soldier soldat *m.*
solemnity solennité *f.*
some (*adj.*) = part. art.; quelque
some (*pron.*) = part. pron.; quelques-uns
something quelque chose *m.*
sometimes quelquefois
son fils *m.*
song chanson *f.*
soon bientôt; as soon as aussitôt que
sorry, to be regretter
sort sorte *f.*
sound son *m.*
soup potage *m.*, soupe *f.*
south sud *m.*
Spain Espagne *f.*
Spaniard Espagnol *m.*
Spanish espagnol
speak parler
special spécial
specialty spécialité *f.*
spectacle spectacle *m.*
spend (time) passer; mettre (à); (money) dépenser
spite, in spite of malgré
splendid splendide
spread étendre
spring printemps *m.*
square place *f.*
square (*adj.*) carré
stable étable *f.*
stained glass window vitrail *m.*, *plu.* vitraux
stairs escalier *m.*
stamp timbre-poste *m.*
stand se tenir debout; être; supporter
star étoile *f.*
start partir; = to begin commencer
starve mourir de faim
state état *m.*
station gare *f.*

statue statue *f.*
stay rester
steal voler
steeple flèche *f.*
step marche *f.*
stick bâton *m.*
still pourtant, cependant
stone pierre *f.*
stop (s')arrêter; descendre; cesser
store magasin *m.*
story histoire *f.*
stove poêle *m.*
strange étrange
street rue *f.*
strength force *f.*
strike frapper
striking (*adj.*) frappant
string bean haricot vert *m.*
student étudiant *m.*
study étudier
stupid bête, stupide
subdivide subdiviser
subject sujet *m.*
sub-prefect sous-préfet *m.*
subscribe s'abonner
suburb banlieue *f.*
subway souterrain *m.*; subway-train train souterrain
succeed réussir
such tel; such a un tel; (*with adj.*) si
sudden, all of a tout d'un coup
suffer souffrir
sum somme *f.*
summer été *m.*
sun soleil *m.*
Sunday dimanche *m.*
sunset coucher (*m.*) du soleil
superb superbe
suppose supposer
sure sûr
surmounted surmonté
surprise étonner, surprendre; to be surprised s'étonner

surround environner
sweep nettoyer
swim nager
Swiss suisse
Switzerland Suisse *f.*
symbolism symbolisme *m.*
system système *m.*

T

table table *f.*
take prendre, conduire, mener; **(carry to)** apporter; **(require time)** falloir; **to take a walk** faire une promenade; **to take place** avoir lieu; **to take care of** garder, prendre garde de
tale conte *m.*
talent talent *m.*
talk parler
tapestry tapisserie *f.*
tea thé *m.*
teach enseigner
teacher professeur *m.*
telegraph télégraphe *m.*
telephone téléphone *m.*
tell dire; **to tell about** parler de; **to tell** (a story) raconter
temple temple *m.*
tennis tennis *m.*
tennis court salle (*f.*) du jeu de paume
term terme *m.*
territory territoire *m.*
thank remercier
thank you merci
thanks to grâce à
that (*conj.*) que
that (see dem. pron.); **that is** c'est-à-dire
thatch chaume *m.*
theater théâtre *m.*
then alors, puis, ensuite
there là, y

thermometer thermomètre *m.*
thesis thèse *f.*
thick épais
thin léger
thing chose *f.*
think penser, croire; trouver
third troisième; **third estate** tiers état
thorn épine *f.*
though: as though comme si
thoroughly à fond
thousand (*collectively*) millier *m.*
thread fil *m.*
threaten menacer
through à travers, au travers de; par (see grammar).
throw jeter
Thursday jeudi
ticket billet *m.*
tide marée *f.*
tightly étroitement
time temps *m.*, heure *f.*; **present time** heure actuelle; = **occasion** fois *f.*; **from time to time** de temps en temps; **in time** à temps; **at the same time** en même temps; **it is time** il est temps; **have a good time** s'amuser; **have such a good time** s'amuser tant, *or* tellement
times (in multiplication table) fois
tip pourboire *m.*
tip (*vb.*) donner un pourboire à
tired fatigué; **to become tired** se lasser
to à
to-day aujourd'hui
together ensemble
tomb tombeau *m.*
to-morrow demain
Tom Thumb le petit Poucet
to-night ce soir

VOCABULARY

too trop; (= also)aussi
top sommet *m.*
" tough " vaurien *m.*
Touring Club Touring Club *m.*
toward vers (physical and time); envers (mental)
tower tour *f.*
town ville *f.*
toy joujou *m.*
trade commerce *m.*
trade (*vb.*) faire des emplettes
tragic tragique
train train *m.*
trained instruit
translate traduire
translation traduction *f.*
travel (*vb.*) voyager
travel (*n.*) voyage *m.*
traveler voyageur *m.*
tree arbre *m.*
trial épreuve *f.*
Trianon Trianon *m.*
trip voyage *m.*, excursion *f.;* parcours *m.*
Trocadero Trocadéro *m.*
trouble peine *f.*
true vrai
trunk malle *f.*
trust se fier à
try essayer
tube tube *m.*
Tuesday mardi *m.*
tulip tulipe *f.*
tunnel tunnel *m.*
turn tour *m.*
turn (*vb.*) tourner
turnip navet *m.*
twelve o'clock midi (noon), minuit (night)
twice deux fois

U

umbrella parapluie *m.*
uncle oncle *m.*
under sous
understand comprendre
unite (s')unir
United States Etats-Unis *m. plu.*
university université *f.*
unless à moins que
unload décharger
until (*prep.*) jusqu'à
until (*conj.*) jusqu'à ce que
up (river) en amont
use employer, se servir de; what is the use of à quoi bon + inf.; to be of no use avoir beau + inf.
used (*adj.*) accoutumé
usual d'ordinaire
usually ordinairement

V

vain, to be in avoir beau + inf.
valley vallée *f.*
value valeur *f.*
vanquished (p. p. of vaincre)
various divers, -es
vassal vassal *m.*
vast vaste
vault caveau *m.*
vegetable végétable *f.*, légume *f.;* **early vegetables** primeurs *f. plu.*
vendor vendeur *m.*, vendeuse *f.*
ventilate ventiler
verb verbe *m.*
very très
very (*adj.*) même (after noun modified)
vessel vaisseau *m.*
victorious vainqueur
view vue *f.*
villa villa *f.*
village village *m.*
violet violette *f.*
virgin vierge *f.*

visit (*vb.*) visiter
visit (*n.*) visite *f.*
voice voix *f.*
volume tome *m.*, volume *m.*
voter votant *m.*

W

wage gage *m.*
wait (for) attendre
wait (*n.*) attente *f.*; **wait between acts** entr'acte *m.*
wake (up) (s')éveiller
walk (*n.*) promenade *f.*; **to take a walk** faire une promenade, se promener
walk (*vb.*) se promener (à pied), marcher; **to walk through** parcourir
wall mur *m.*
want vouloir
war guerre *f.*
warm chaud; **to be warm (weather)** faire chaud; **to be warm (person)** avoir chaud
warm (*vb.*) chauffer
wash laver
wash house, washing place lavoir *m.*
washing lessive *f.*
waste perdre
water eau *f.*
way manière *f.*; (= **road**) chemin *m.*; **to find one's way about** s'orienter; **on the way (to)** en route (pour); **by the way** par exemple
weak faible
wear porter
weather temps *m.*
week semaine *f.*
well bien; eh bien!; **as well** (= **likewise**) également; **as well as** ainsi que

west ouest *m.*
wet mouiller
wharf quai *m.*
what (see rel. and interr. pron.); **what of it!** qu'importe!
whatever (*pron.*) quoi que
whatever (*adj.*) quelque . . . que
wheat blé *m.*
wheel roue *f.*
when quand, lorsque
whence d'où
whenever quand, toutes les fois que
where où
whether si; **whether . . . or** soit que . . . ou que
which (see rel. and interr. pron. and interr. adj.)
while pendant que; tandis que
while (*n.*) quelque temps; **after a while** après un peu
white blanc
whitewashed blanchi (à chaux)
who, whom, whose (see rel. and interr. pron.)
whole entier
why pourquoi; **why!** mais!
wide large; **wide open** grand ouvert
widow veuve *f.*
wife femme *f.*
wild sauvage
will (*vb.*) vouloir
will (*n.*) testament *m.*
William Guillaume
willing, to be vouloir bien
wind serrer
wind vent *m.*
window fenêtre *f.*; **store window** vitrine *f.*
windy, to be faire du vent
wine vin *m.*
winter hiver *m.*

VOCABULARY

Wise Men mages *m. plu.*
wish vouloir
with avec, de (see grammar)
within dans, en
without sans
woman femme *f.*
wonder se demander; s'étonner; **it is no wonder** ce n'est pas étonnant
wonderful merveilleux
wood bois *m.*
wooden de bois
woods bois *m.*
word mot *m.*
work (*vb.*) travailler
work (*n.*) travail *m.*, œuvre *f.*
working (*adj.*) ouvrier
workman ouvrier *m.*
world monde *m.*
worth, to be valoir; **to be worth while** valoir la peine, être la peine
wrap serrer
write écrire
writing écriture *f.*
wrong, to be avoir tort

Y

yard cour *f.*
year an *m.*, année *f.*
yellow jaune
yes oui
yesterday hier
yet encore
young jeune
your votre

Z

zero zéro *m.*

LE FRANÇAIS ET SA PATRIE

With Notes and Vocabulary

BY

L. RAYMOND TALBOT, A.M.

INSTRUCTOR IN ROMANCE LANGUAGES IN BOSTON UNIVERSITY

TEACHERS of French have long felt the need of a first-year reader which is easy, interesting and instructive. Fairy tales do not appeal to the average pupil; neither do the morbid stories which are found in readers of the ordinary type. Moreover, these stories do not inspire any admiration for French literature.

Mr. Talbot has written his own experiences in a bright, entertaining style, in easy, colloquial, idiomatic French. The book teems with information of value also to advanced classes which wish to study the life of the people whose language and literature they know. Incidentally, the book furnishes an excellent working vocabulary which teachers welcome as a basis for conversation.

The first part of the book is in the form of **Conversations**. Two young Americans in visiting Paris, one of them for the first time, comment upon French meals, transportation facilities, theatres, postal services, Sunday observance, buying books, and so on.

The second part is in the form of **Letters** describing Paris and customs which lend themselves more readily to this form of description than to conversation. In the springtime, when the country is most worthy of the title "la belle France," the author made long trips in Normandy, Brittany, the Loire Valley, and Provence.

A few of the choicest French poems and a half-dozen songs give the student a glimpse of priceless treasures which may be his if he pursues the study of French beyond the first year.

The book contains two maps, showing only places mentioned in the text, and many illustrations, some of which are from photographs taken by the author.

In two years "Le Français et sa Patrie" went through five editions, and was adopted in nearly 1000 schools. The present edition profits from various suggestions made by teachers in both countries.

Correspondence Solicited

BENJ. H. SANBORN & CO.

CHICAGO   ✤ ✤   NEW YORK   ✤ ✤   BOSTON